The 9 Intense Experiences

The 9 Intense Experiences

An Action Plan to Change Your Life Forever

BRIAN VASZILY

WILEY

John Wiley & Sons, Inc.

Library of Congress Cataloging-in-Publication Data:
Vaszily, Brian, date.
  The 9 intense experiences : an action plan to change your life forever / Brian Vaszily.
      p. cm.
  Includes bibliographical references and index.
  ISBN 978-0-470-59635-7 (hardback : acid-free paper))
  1. Self-actualization (Psychology)   2. Change (Psychology)   I. Title.   II. Title: Nine intense experiences.
  BF637.S4V38 2011
  158—dc22

                                                                    2010045248

Dedicated to my mother, Maryann Vaszily. Scholars, authors, doctors, artists, and sages have guided me and I am grateful, but they don't hold a candle to you. You live the knowledge, you live love, and that has been by far the greatest lesson. Thank you.

This time, like all times, is a very good one if we but know what to do with it.

—Ralph Waldo Emerson

Contents

An Important Note for Doubters and Skimmers

This book will have you laughing out loud, crying to yourself, getting lost, dreaming vividly, giving stuff you love away, and running around in your underwear. It is unlike any other book you've ever experienced, but don't let that stop you. It will change the course of your life in powerful and positive ways. And it will do so rapidly. You will soon see why the profound changes I am promising that you will discover with *The 9 Intense Experiences* are natural and inevitable.

If you are seeking to overcome barriers to your happiness and success, such as fear, guilt, anger, depression, heartbreak, low self-esteem, apathy, feeling overwhelmed, and not knowing the direction to take in life, this book will inevitably help you. If you want to achieve greater success in your career, love life and other relationships, health, weight, finances, or all of these, this book will guide you in powerful ways you can't yet imagine.

In today's go-go, faster-faster, feel-as-if-you-are-getting-nowhere world, many people tend to believe they have visited and know a lake, when in reality their eyes have only skimmed the surface of that lake. We're in an age of skimming life when we were born to dive deep, and that causes a painful disconnection from the success, happiness, and inner peace we are meant to have. That is precisely the disease that this book cures.

A term I often use for this problem is the "Muddy Slope Syndrome"—when you have it, you feel as if life is an uphill climb in the pouring rain, and you're moving faster and faster and digging in deeper and deeper, trying to get up that hill. The faster you move and the deeper you dig in, the muddier that slope gets, and you slip farther and farther backward. You feel increasingly weighed down and blinded by the mud splattering all over you.

Please do yourself a giant favor: take a few deep breaths and slow down long enough to read just a bit more of this book. Slow down the way you slow down to kiss your lover, the way you slow down to eat really good chocolate, or the way you slow down to savor whatever you already know gives your life vibrancy.

After reading just a few more sections, you will understand why this book will inevitably change the course of your life in powerful and positive ways. It will make perfect sense. You'll also have more than a few big "aha!" moments that will immediately provide you with greater energy, clarity, and focus, and there's nothing wrong with a little instant gratification!

"We are constantly invited to be who we are," Thoreau wrote. Deep inside, you already know who you are. If you can see yourself achieving greater happiness and success in your relationships, finances, health and weight, career, and elsewhere in your life—that is who you already are. You cannot see something that is not there.

The challenge comes from clearing through the "rust and crust"—another phrase I often use to describe the years and decades of self-sabotaging habits, thoughts, and emotions that paralyze your ability to be, and sometimes even see, who you are.

As you will shortly discover, intense experiences are precisely how to clear through all of that rust and crust. So dive deeper. Accept the invitation to finally be who you know you really are. Life is way too short not to. Now is the time. You absolutely deserve it. And by the way, you're going to love it.

Preface: An Unusual Phone Call to My Father

I've pulled into a strip mall parking lot. The rain beats on my car windows, and the steam from my breath makes them hazier still.

"Hey, Dad, it's Brian," I say into my cell phone. There's no need for a phone, but it helps with this connection. I swallow hard. "It's been a long time."

It is 2002. A decade ago my first wife, Mireya, was twenty-three, I was twenty-two, and we were raising our one-and-a-half-year-old son. We were both full-time college students and working minimum-wage jobs. We were deep in debt, on food stamps and welfare, and living in an apartment smaller than some closets. When Mireya got pregnant in 1990, we had been dating for only four months. At age twenty, when I discovered that I was going to be a father, my own father had already been on his deathbed for three months in a hospital. Prior to that, he'd been dying for more a decade at home from emphysema, alcoholism, depression, and bitterness.

Dad lived what his World War II buddies would have called one hell of a life—high highs and very low lows. He was born in Brooklyn but raised on a sugar beet farm in Hungary by an aunt who often beat him. He moved back to Brooklyn, where he boxed, played handball, and indulged his passion for learning languages. He spoke several by the time he enlisted in the U.S. Army. By the end of his life, he spoke at least seven fluently. He served in intelligence during World War II, doing secret work throughout Europe. During the war, he fell in love with a Russian spy. One day she disappeared, and he never heard anything about her again. He eventually fell in love again and married. During an argument with this first wife early in their marriage, she was hit and killed by a vehicle. Over the years, he launched several businesses, including a restaurant, import/export companies, and other ventures. He married again; his second marriage ended in divorce. Several years later, when I was three, his thirteen-year-old son from this second marriage was also hit and killed by a vehicle.

My mother was his third wife; she was married to him for the final twenty-five years of his life. She primarily supported us on her secretary's salary for the last ten or so years. She tells me he was a very good man when he was healthy—kind, funny, and brilliant. I remember the humor and the brilliance, which often surfaced during his final years. I recall his kindness, too, but these memories are far fewer, because I grew up while the unresolved tragedies of his life ground down his mind, body, and spirit. He largely turned into somebody he was not. When I was around age nine, he became a severe alcoholic. He was often cruel to my mom, my sister, and me. Our paranoid nights of not knowing when he'd come home and what he would do this time finally abated when he eventually quit drinking; it was quit or die, and to his credit, he did stop. Yet his severe and unresolved self-bitterness, and using us as his outlet for it, did not abate. Mine is a story that many others have told before, one that far too many people have experienced: routine belittlement, vile names, being told countless times that his pain and emotional abuse of my mom and sister were my fault.

In 1990, my father was in the hospital for months, dying a horrible death. My mother worked at her secretarial job during the day, fought the inept medical system in the evenings, and at night tended to my father at his bedside. My sister and I spent many nights in the waiting room. I recall a pastor at the hospital pulling me aside and whispering, "You'd better take care of your mom, or she's going to end up in the bed next to your dad." That was shortly after I learned that my girlfriend of four months was pregnant. I was a twenty-year-old child who was going to be a father, my own father was dying, and I hadn't confronted any of the years of issues with him. It was a perfect storm of guilt and blame. I felt responsible for his suffering and dying. I felt responsible for the shattered relationship between us and for my mom's and sister's suffering as he died. Because my girlfriend came from a Mexican family and she believed that some of the stricter members would ostracize her for bearing our child out of wedlock, and because I didn't want to cause anyone in this world any more pain, I asked her to marry me. I didn't even believe in marriage then. I barely even knew her.

After six months in the hospital, on August 9, 1990, my father died. On December 1, 1990, I got married. On January 30, 1991, I turned twenty-one. On February 28, 1991, my son was born. We lived for several months in a small studio apartment in Chicago, sleeping on two twin mattresses on the floor, where I'd awaken at night to the sensation of mice whiskers tickling my face. We spent several other months living with my mom—my wife, the baby, and I all crammed into my childhood bedroom, where the same moon and star stickers I had pasted to the ceiling as a boy still glowed at night. By September 1991, we were both working and were full-time college students living with our baby on campus at Northern Illinois University.

By the middle of 1992, with a couple of years to go before graduation, we owed tens of thousands of dollars in student loans and thousands more in credit card bills. We were on food stamps and briefly on welfare. Each month we struggled to pay our bills; on multiple occasions, I sold music CDs I had collected over the years to secondhand stores to keep our lights on, until I had depleted my entire treasured music collection. I vowed that after we graduated in 1994, I would never be in that position again.

᠀

Back now to 2002. I am in tears, parked in the car in the rain and making this cell phone call. My first wife and I had divorced, and I remarried. My son lives with us half of the time and my stepdaughter lives with us full-time. A couple of years earlier, I worked hard to land a good-paying job in a dot-com startup. I bought my first home and started to dig myself out of the debt I'd acquired over the years. Then the dot-com folded. I was laid off. While I searched for jobs, my severance package dried up. I started to receive unemployment benefits. I had a well-reviewed novel published, but it didn't pay the bills. I went bankrupt. Then September 11, 2001, occurred, and it changed me in profound ways (more about that later).

The economy crashed after 9/11. After sending out hundreds of résumés, I still had no job. My unemployment compensation ran out. I had also drained my meager retirement fund. We were living on my wife's small income from her private school job. It didn't cover the mortgage, much less our other bills. I had accepted a part-time job as a waiter. It still wouldn't come close to paying our bills, and I had to swallow my pride after the critical success of my novel and working hard for years after college to get somewhere in the business world. Just prior to accepting that part-time waiter job, I had sold most of my music CD collection to a secondhand store—CDs I had acquired since selling off my first collection ten years earlier—to keep our lights on.

I am back where I vowed ten years ago I'd never be again. I have no idea how we're going to keep the house and eat, much less pay other bills. But that's not why I have broken down, driven into the strip-mall parking lot, and pulled out my phone. I am in tears because I realize that I yearn for an older, wiser man to turn to for some guidance, calm reassurance, or get-tougher-damn-it advice. The only person I can think to call is my dead father.

"Hey, Dad, it's Brian." I swallow hard. "It's been a long time." I imagine his voice, the voice I recall from his kind periods: deep, confident, sober.

"Brian, just please know I became someone I was not," I hear him say. "Something I was not. There are many reasons, but I have no excuses."

Sobs explode from my chest until I can barely breathe. I force it out: "What the hell am I supposed to do? You're my father, you were supposed to be there for me, not fuck me over, you bastard! And you're supposed to be here for me now! What the hell am I supposed to do?"

The phone against my ear is now silent. I am shouting to myself. This is all just made up. Stupid. The rain has softened to a pattering against the car windows. My eyes follow a single droplet that starts at the top of the windshield and winds its way down until it becomes part of the pool at the base of the window.

"You're doing what you are supposed to be doing." Though my father's voice in the phone is calm, it still surprises me. "Brian, you are confronting me." And there in my car in the strip-mall lot in the rain, I finally hear my father. I finally get to listen to the real Dad. Not the mean drunk, not the asshole, but my dad. I hear him tell me many things. He says I have done quite well, considering. He tells me to forgive myself for mistakes I've made, such as cheating on my first wife when I was younger, angry, and more ignorant. He tells me I will make many more mistakes during my life, but the key is to let the mistakes teach me, not swallow me. I hear him tell me there is nothing wrong with being afraid, that I will fear things for the rest of my life, but there is a world of difference between feeling fear and letting it control me. "You cannot outrun or hide from fear, Brian," he says. "It will always catch you from behind, eager to consume you. Keep confronting your fear, just as you are doing right now by finally talking to me."

I ask him questions about his life, but he tells me that is only secondary to what matters now. What matters now is that I have something important to give the world, something that can really help people. He says I shouldn't think for a moment about giving up what I am building. "There never comes a point, Brian, when any life is clear of challenges, so don't fall into the trap of waiting for that impossible point to pursue your dreams. Stop at nothing to give the world what you have to give. Starting now," I hear him say, "always starting now." I hear him tell me I was just a child when he was so cruel, that his alcoholism and cruelty and my mother's and sister's pain were not my fault. I hear him tell me that he knows I will help make the world a better place. I hear him tell me, for the first time, that he believes in me. "Brian," he says, "I am sorry. I am so very sorry."

I know he is. "It's okay, Dad." And that is the truth, the start of okay.

"I love you, Son," I hear his voice say. I realize that I believe him. I tell him I love him, too. Then I close the phone and pocket it.

Things are clearer. Things are going to be okay. I start the car and drive away.

Part I

✺

How to Become Who You Know You Really Are

The purpose of life is to live it, to taste experience to the utmost, to reach out eagerly and without fear for newer and richer experience.

—*Eleanor Roosevelt*

I have now reigned about 50 years in victory or peace, beloved by my subjects, dreaded by my enemies, and respected by my allies. Riches and honors, power and pleasure, have waited on my call, nor does any earthly blessing appear to have been wanting to my felicity. In this situation, I have diligently numbered the days of pure and genuine happiness which have fallen to my lot. They amount to fourteen.

—*Abd Er-Rahman III of Spain (960 C.E.)*

How we spend our days is, of course, how we spend our lives.

—*Annie Dillard*

What Life Do You Envision for Yourself?

I ntense Experiences are not limited to scaling Mount Everest or taking a year off to wander the globe. Those certainly can be transformative experiences, but they are not what this book will provide. You may want monumental experiences like those, and if so, I hope you get to do them, but you don't need them to rapidly and extensively change your life.

Intense Experiences are captivating, energizing, and revealing journeys inside yourself that will clear through your barriers and positively transform you as nothing else can. These journeys engage your mind, body, heart, and spirit. In varying senses of the words, you'll also find that Intense Experiences are both enjoyable and deeply satisfying.

They're also easy, in the sense that you don't have to spend excessive amounts of time, energy, money, or willpower to pursue them. You don't have to take time off from your job. You don't have to invest in special gadgets. You don't have to push your brain or body or struggle in any way to engage in these Intense Experiences and achieve their inevitable benefits.

Those who have already gone through Intense Experiences via my training say that the experiences feel "natural," "real," "right," and "in tune with my being" because, as you will shortly discover, they absolutely are.

As for their inevitable ability to transform you, they won't change you into something you are not. Nothing can do that, and there's no need for you to become something you are not, anyway. Instead, Intense Experiences will transform you into who you really are—into who, deep inside, you already know or will soon discover you are meant to be.

This will happen whatever your age or circumstance; for example, perhaps you already know in your core that you were meant to be wealthy or healthier. Or to successfully run a certain business, soar to far greater heights in your career, or make people's lives better with your music, writing, healing therapies, or whatever passions and gifts reside within you. Perhaps you know in your core that you are meant to be more satisfied in a love relationship or have a better relationship with your children, parents, work mates, or friends.

Judging from the thousands of people I have guided and corresponded with—and from many studies such as the American Psychological Association's annual study on stress, which shows increasing and alarmingly high numbers of people who claim that they are stressed out, exhausted, depressed, and irritated—it is likely that you already know in your core that you were meant to feel considerably more energy, inner peace, clarity, and overall life satisfaction than you currently do.

A big caution: in today's sprint-paced and negativity-saturated world, it is way too easy to get jaded and assume that you're fooling yourself about ever achieving these states of being and your goals and dreams. Maybe you sometimes think, I don't have enough time, and that you should "get real" and "settle for" your current lot in life; perhaps certain other people tend to provoke you into these self-sabotaging thoughts.

Here's what that is: nonsense. Worse than that—it is deadly.

When you give up the pursuit of your dreams and happiness and settle for mediocre or worse, you join the walking dead. You are here to live deeply and richly, not to get caught in a rut and rot away.

Whatever you envision for yourself, it not only *can be*, but in the most important sense it *already is*. As grandiose or flighty as some jaded folks may say it sounds, you cannot see and feel what is not already there. And despite what our society's overworked mentality may have everyone believe, the most crucial step in becoming who you know you are meant to be is *not* in working harder and longer hours to get there. If you are like most adults today, you already work too much, certainly more than many people who have achieved great life satisfaction and their biggest goals and dreams—those who live the Intense Experiences that you are about to live, too.

Instead, the first step is clearing away the years of rust and crust that have accrued inside you and paralyzed you, as a result of all of your self-doubt, fear, anger, guilt, sadness, distrust, fatigue, and more. Notice that I am not saying you should avoid these negative feelings; they are a part of life, and they can even have their benefits. The key is learning to recognize, embrace, and then ultimately let those emotions go, versus allowing them to build up self-paralyzing rust and crust inside you.

This is one of the most important things that the 9 Intense Experiences do. These unique journeys transform you into who you know you really are by enabling you to both recognize and clear through all of the rust and the crust that's holding you down. As nothing else can, they cure your paralysis.

In my "Unusual Phone Call to My Father" from the preface, I didn't suddenly become something that I was not. Instead, this experience helped make me aware of, and start to clear through, some barriers that were holding me back from being who I really am.

As you will discover, both well-known and little-known people who have achieved happiness, inner peace, and their greatest goals all share this in common: they routinely engage in positive Intense Experiences, specifically in nine crucial areas of experience.

Meanwhile, most people suffering from Muddy Slope Syndrome have forgotten or never discovered the unparalleled transformative power of engaging in Intense Experiences in the first place.

Congratulations, you are about to discover it.

A Crucial Question for You

I'm about to ask you an important question. But to frame it properly, you should know that in my past I've worked extensively with several of today's most respected dietary health and wellness experts, from coauthoring, editing, and agenting their books to managing their newsletters, Web sites, and more. Here, in convenient capsule form, is what they primarily teach: you are what you eat.

Eat primarily organic vegetables, probiotic-rich foods, and naturally raised meats, and drink clean water and green tea, and you'll get a healthy body out of it. Exercise regularly and things are even better.

Or, instead, eat lots of Twinkies, and you'll get a body that looks and feels like a Twinkie. Don't exercise and things will be even worse: you'll look and feel like a deep-fried Twinkie dipped in sugar.

Yet although this makes perfect sense—a healthy diet and exercise are certainly important—it is only part of the equation you need to follow to achieve peak energy, creativity, clarity, peace, and happiness and, for that matter, physical health and longevity. And it is not even the most crucial part.

Many people with some type of disease have still lived rich and satisfying lives, achieving their greatest goals and happiness, by addressing the most elemental part of the equation. (In fact, by addressing it, they often find far greater success at permanently maintaining a healthy diet and exercise!)

On the flip side, many people who are fiercely dedicated to a proper diet and exercise still feel overwhelmed, fatigued, stressed out, depressed, or as if they just aren't achieving the success and satisfaction they know they are meant to. That is because they have not addressed the most important part of the health and happiness equation.

That crucial part is emotional health. Mental clarity. Being true to your spirit. It goes by many names, but it is the deep and steady awareness that you are firmly centered in who you really are. You know that you are on the right path to be and achieve what you are meant to in life. You have the clarity and the humbleness to embrace less-than-enjoyable emotions while also recognizing the barriers in your way and the desire and the resolve to keep dissolving those barriers.

Some of the most common barriers include feeling fatigued, stressed out, short on time, confused, angry, hurt, afraid, depressed, lonely, misunderstood, and ignored, and letting these emotions control you. Some challenging emotions are of course inevitable in life. As the Emmy Award–winning talk show host Montel Williams, who has battled multiple sclerosis for years, noted in his wonderful book *Living Well Emotionally*, such challenges "can help us grow, and become stronger, and change ourselves for the better." It is not about trying to eliminate such emotional challenges from life altogether; that notion is a dangerous mirage. It is when you don't properly manage them and try to ignore them, defeat them through willpower or quick fixes like so many self-help fads, or mask them with excessive work, alcohol, drugs, or shopping, that they become major barriers.

They block you from the happiness, inner peace, and success you envision for yourself and therefore are meant to have, in your career, health, finances, relationships, and every area of your life.

So it's time to ask you the crucial question: *What are you putting into your being?*

Because you are not just what you eat. You are what you spend your time and energy doing. You are the experiences you take part in. What you invite into your being—into your mind, heart, body, and spirit—through your eyes, ears, nose, mouth, and skin on a routine basis, *is* who you will be.

If you keep doing whatever it is you spend your time and energy doing in life, if you keep inviting the same experiences in that you always do, you will keep getting what you've got. You will naturally stay exactly where you are in life, unless some outside force—winning the lottery or, far more likely, some tragedy like a serious disease—finally shoves your life elsewhere for you.

Over the years I've worked with many people one on one, and I've corresponded with participants in my seminars, thousands of readers of my IntenseExperiences.com newsletter, and many more people in my consulting and coaching work. I have often asked these people for a breakdown on what they usually spend their waking hours *doing*, and here is the typical answer:

Working a lot. Listening to the radio in the car if they drive to and from work—typically, the news, talk shows, or Top 40 music. Getting some exercise if they're one of the fitness-focused ones. And, in whatever "spare time" they have, including evenings and weekends, watching prime-time shows and quite a bit of other TV. Making food or eating out. Running errands. Shopping, shopping, and more shopping. Surfing the Internet, primarily for more news, for information on how to fix their health and lives—and for more shopping. Maybe, if they can squeeze it in occasionally, going to the movies or the beach, indulging in a hobby like gardening, or even reading magazines and books a little. And did I mention working, TV, and shopping?

The Princeton economist Alan B. Krueger and the Nobel laureate Daniel Kahneman recently led a major project in which four thousand Americans were interviewed about how they typically spend their day. The findings succinctly reflect my own informal findings noted earlier: people usually spend only about 17 percent of their day engaged in highly enjoyable and meaningful activities such as spiritual practices, listening to music, and exercising. They spend an additional 11.5 percent of the day engaged in moderately enjoyable activities like walking and talking on the phone to friends and loved ones.

I wouldn't even call all of the activities the researchers grouped into these categories Intense Experiences; some are, whereas others are not necessarily transformative but are at least enjoyable. That said, it should be obvious that when the average American spends only about 28.5 percent of his or her day on enjoyable and/or meaningful experiences, something is drastically wrong.

If your diet consists of only 28.5 percent healthy foods, obviously you are in for some serious health issues. If you contribute only 28.5 percent of positive and meaningful work to your job, you will soon be fired.

Yet there is this false but prevalent sense in the Western world today that life has to be hard or you're doing something wrong. There's this sense that you have to feel fatigued and beaten down every day to get brownie points from God, Dad, your boss, or some authority figure lording it over you. People are largely ignoring the fact that they are starving to death for positive and transformative experiences.

It really is the most sinister and deadly epidemic of our time, because it kills individual and collective energy, creativity, clarity, focus, hope, passion, and drive to do things that make your life and our world a happier place. Therefore, it also kills the ability to resolve other issues— on a personal scale, the emotional barriers I spoke of earlier, and on a grand scale, societal issues such as wars, the economy, the environment, racism, poverty, and disease epidemics—that stand in the way of making your life and our world a much happier place.

What are you putting into your being? What experiences are you engaging in that are good for you? That are not good for you? Which ones should you be engaging in that you are not, much to the detriment of your health and happiness?

If you eat lots of Twinkies, you are going to look and feel like a Twinkie. Likewise, if you engage in lots of empty and toxic experiences, you will look and feel empty and toxic. Feeling that way certainly won't enable you to dissolve the barriers to your happiness and success.

If you instead engage in captivating, enjoyable, deeply satisfying, and transformative experiences, also known as Intense Experiences, you will feel far more energy, clarity, creativity, focus, passion, and drive to do what you know deep inside you are meant to do. To be who you really are.

I started researching and developing the Intense Experiences program well before I heard of the now-booming field of positive psychology. When I did discover everything that researchers such as Martin Seligman, Mihály Csíkszentmihályi, Barbara Fredrickson, and Todd Kashdan were doing, I was positively blown away.

For most of their history, traditional psychological research and application have focused on finding and fixing problems. Positive psychology instead focuses on "the strengths and virtues that enable individuals and communities to thrive." Enabling you to thrive, not merely survive, is what the 9 Intense Experiences is all about. While thousands of people have already been transformed through the experiences you will encounter here in my training, the extensive research in the exciting field of positive psychology—and also in the booming and equally groundbreaking field of neuroscience—has helped lay a strong scientific foundation for the transformations you will experience with this book.

Meanwhile, the recent widespread popularity of *The Law of Attraction* and related books such as *The Secret* has certainly opened mainstream minds about the importance of taking control of your own life if you want to experience positive change. *The Law of Attraction* essentially states that it's all about where you focus your mind. And that "if you really want something and truly believe it's possible, you'll get it," but putting a lot of attention and thought into something you don't want means you'll probably get that, too.

Many in the scientific community have fiercely disputed this "law," noting that empirical studies show no proof of this (and when those in the movement do cite "evidence," they do so anecdotally and very self-selectively). Furthermore, scientists state that electrical signals put out by the brain and by thinking are negligible at best. Even some of the leading figures in *The Law of Attraction* movement (and Oprah) have now acknowledged the limits of *The Law of Attraction*.

Although not necessarily in the physical sense of altering events outside of your own being, I do believe that where your thoughts are focused has an impact on your own reality. Yet to rely on driving your life in the direction you want it to go by focusing your thoughts on it would take impossible amounts of your time and energy and leave you with little time for anything else. In our order-it-now-and-it-appears culture, it is tempting to believe that some focused thinking here and there within our sixteen to seventeen hours per day of being awake will change our lives. It can certainly help, but if you reflect on your own day-to-day life, you will realize that you spend most of your time *doing*.

Whether you are working, playing on the beach, watching news, talking on the phone, gardening, or reading this book, the *experiences* you are engaged in drive your thoughts, emotions, and general sense of well-being or lack thereof.

You cannot possibly, nor do you have to, struggle to focus your mind throughout your daily life to become who you know you really are. The experiences you invite into your being—into your mind, heart, body, and spirit—through your eyes, ears, nose, mouth, and skin on a routine basis are who you will be.

What are you putting into your being?

The amazing field of positive psychology has established the scientific foundation for this concept. The success of *The Law of Attraction* has opened the door wider for people to take control of their own lives. Intense Experiences will inevitably take you where you know you are meant to go.

In the next part of this book, you will discover why you already know this is true at your core, although you may have consciously forgotten or never learned it in the first place.

You've Already Had Intense Experiences But . . .

I n the years I've spent researching Intense Experiences, I discovered that there are nine key areas of experience that remarkably happy and successful people focus their time and energy on that other individuals do not.

By remarkably happy and successful, I don't just mean in the sense of being wealthy, although often that is a by-product of their success. What I mean is that they've accomplished many of their greatest goals, they're always actively reaching for more, challenges may sidetrack them but never break who they are, they're quite content with—but never stagnant in—their lives, and they radiate positive energy and tend to smile a lot.

Some of these people are alive today. Some of them you may know of, others you don't. Many others are successful "people for all time." That's a nice way of saying that you have likely heard their names before, they left some kind of positive impression on the world, while proclaiming a deep satisfaction with their lives, but they are now dead.

An essential point worth repeating is this: what primarily separates these successful and deeply satisfied people from everyone else is not that they work harder. Many people work hard their whole lives and never achieve their biggest goals and dreams.

Many remarkably successful people, meanwhile, don't work nearly as hard as you do.

These people may not have been born wealthy or had any type of advantage in life that others don't have. Many successful people were in fact born dirt poor and met with great tragedies, while others who have been given all of the advantages in the world are nonetheless miserable.

What separates these happy, successful people from others is that they dedicate time, energy, and intention to doing things within these nine areas that everyone else has become too distracted to know, understand, and experience. They don't remain focused on all of these areas of experience, but they do focus on many of these areas. After you read this book, you, too, will likely discover a preference for channeling your time and energy into certain experience areas more than into others.

Which leads to one of the most important points of all:

> You have already had Intense Experiences in your life. They have shaped your life. Everyone has had Intense Experiences in life.

The problem, however, is that nearly everyone except for the aforementioned happy and successful people has forgotten or never consciously learned the extreme importance of intentionally engaging in such experiences.

As I mentioned earlier, most adults today are—to varying degrees of severity, and only you can assess your own degree—seemingly caught in ruts of mind-, heart-, spirit- and happiness-numbing routine. The rust and crust developed from years and decades of going faster, working harder, avoiding deep human interactions, and seeking but never really finding solace in shopping, drinking, and other mirages of coping barricade them from realizing the inevitably transformative power of such experiences.

Every single day, many positive and potentially transformative experiences present themselves to us. Things as simple as initiating a more-than-just-small-talk discussion with that stranger sitting next to you at lunch, who may end up changing your life, or delving into a book like this versus watching another reality TV show. Most people don't even recognize these experiences, however, much less embrace them. (And kudos to you for seeking out this book; you obviously get it!)

Toward the end of 2008, I asked readers of my Intense Experiences newsletter to post in one of my blogs a positive Intense Experience that, in their adult lives, changed them in ways small or large. Nearly a thousand people posted their experiences (you can read their responses at IntenseExperiences.com), and many of them added that they were surprised to realize that these Intense Experiences, these unparalleled opportunities for growth, really do exist so abundantly in their lives.

Intense Experiences are constantly presenting themselves, but people are so focused on their ruts that they don't even see them. As a result, there are only two types of Intense Experiences that people typically allow to affect their lives:

1. Those from their childhood
2. The tragic Intense Experiences

Childhood is full of Intense Experiences. Our youthful years are not primarily composed of our intending or willing things to be so. We don't intend to discover how to make our way in the world by playing, for example. We simply play, we do, we are curious, we dive right in, and we discover many revelations we never previously knew about the world and especially about ourselves by doing so.

Our childhood and teenage years consist of immersing ourselves in new experiences and learning and growing from them. Virtually everyone does this with relative abandon when he or she is young, not overanalyzing all of the potential repercussions of that first kiss or of taking a new way home.

Right now, for example, I am writing this in a Starbucks coffee shop. There is a five-year-old boy here, and he has been periodically peeking over my laptop to see what I am doing. And hiding behind a pole in front of me, at which point I act like I don't see him. And placing his sunglasses on that same pole and talking to them as if they are a person. And coloring a placemat. Creating designs on the table with napkins. Building things with the sugar packets. He's curious, he's allowing his creativity to flow, he's not struggling to manifest some desire or force his will on things. At his own five-year-old level, he's simply engaged in Intense Experiences. He's delving into the new, enjoying it, and most certainly growing from it right before my eyes. It's a beautiful thing.

This is the same trait you'll see in remarkably successful and happy people: they don't allow themselves to get trapped in too much routine, in ruts, in too many "have-to-do-its" at the expense of living their lives and becoming who they really are. Within all or some of the nine areas of experience, they keep trying and doing new things, pushing their own boundaries, to discover and achieve.

I have had the privilege of talking to the eighty-something-year-old Louise Hay, the successful author and founder of Hay House Publishing, and she emphatically noted that the key to her success and happiness (and her vibrancy, which still blows away the energy levels of many people half her age) is her commitment to learning and doing new things. Rock on to 120 years of age please, Louise!

Although we all had youthful years loaded with Intense Experiences, most people "grow up"—I'd argue that many more of them get ground down—and they stop having virtually any other form of Intense Experience, save one: the tragic kind.

Which leads me to a question I've often been asked in interviews: How did you come up with the Intense Experiences concept?

Years before I gave them the name Intense Experiences, I started to get glimpses and then longer peeks at the underlying principles that would become the program. My uncle Rod, who writes song lyrics, wrote one called "I'm Not Livin' My Own Life" when I was a child, and I realized even in my later teens that his sentiment seemed to apply to most adults.

As external events go, though, it was 9/11 that primarily led to the creation of Intense Experiences. I experienced 9/11 the way that most people in the United States and many other countries did. I watched it on TV—the planes slamming into the towers, the Pentagon in flames, the towers collapsing, and the wreckage on the field in Pennsylvania. My heart and my mind went in the same two directions that almost everyone's did. One direction was fear of, and anger at, whoever did this and a desire for retribution. Yet the other direction was toward my own loved ones: knowing that could have been any plane, any building, and anyone I care about in those planes and buildings, in all senses of the term I embraced my friends and loved ones much tighter. On a mass scale that I had never witnessed before, almost all of us did.

Witnessing horror and devastation on that scale and realizing how that could have been any of us, any of the people we care about, and recognizing how precious life is, we embraced what really matters in our lives far more tightly than before. I watched as people became more focused on their biggest goals and dreams and not nearly as concerned with the small, insignificant stuff—for a while.

But then the small, insignificant stuff crept back into most people's lives and consumed them again and shoved the things that matter the most off to the side. Paris Hilton and Britney Spears reappeared on our TV sets and in our magazines as if they were something worth focusing on. Committing time to our passions, our loved ones, and our biggest goals and dreams increasingly lost ground once again. That really drove home the question that had been lingering deep inside me even years before 9/11.

It is impossible to pinpoint the date this question first surfaced, because my story reads the way yours may read, too: in my life, I have faced a significant amount of what is commonly known as personal tragedy (but that I like to call, though sometimes only long after the fact, "hard gifts").

You've already learned about one of those situations regarding my relationship with my father. I've also been through two divorces, one difficult and the other very difficult. In my close family on my mother's side, I've had two uncles die young and less than two years apart—one via an instant heart attack and the other through an excruciating form of cancer. And I've witnessed my grandmother, their mother, live through it. I grew up in a rough part of Chicago where I was mugged and beaten up and had my life threatened multiple times, and where young friends of mine joined gangs and were killed. I've experienced what most people would agree are some strange and potentially "paranormal" events. I almost lost one close friend to cancer. Another good friend was killed in a car accident.

I am not citing all of this so that you will pull out the violins for me (although I do enjoy classical music and the occasional fiddle hoedown). On the contrary, keep your violins in their cases, unless you want to play a happy tune, because I know you have experienced your own share of hardships and tragedies in life as well. Aside from wishing that my father, uncles, and old friends were still physically on this earth, I don't wish anything had been different, and I don't feel one bit sorry for myself.

Tragedy and hardship happen, and we can either let them create more tragedy by taking us down, or we can go through the necessary grieving, embrace the pain and other emotions and learn from them, and ultimately view these experiences as sad and difficult but as gifts nonetheless.

The point of my citing these particular challenges is to set up the question that had been building inside me even before September 11, 2001. The 9/11 attacks, though, prompted me to focus deeply and succinctly on this question: once we hit our adult years, is it only tragic Intense Experiences, such as facing serious diseases, the death of loved ones, divorce, and collective events like 9/11 and economic recession, that can realign us to focus on what really matters most in our lives—our biggest goals and dreams, our loved ones, our passions?

Yes, if you make it through serious challenges and tragedies, they will enlighten you—at least for a while, for some people—and will prompt you to recognize and focus on what is really worth pursuing and dedicating your energy to in life. Countless biographies of people who have faced far greater challenges, tragedies, and horrors than I did testify to that.

Yet it seems that for most adults today, it is only these tragic Intense Experiences (if they make it through) that realign them. And often those people are realigned only for a while. Some have even suggested that in a strange subconscious way, people may invite certain types of new tragedies into their lives because these are the only things that adults today allow to realign them to what really matters and to who they really are.

It is not that positive Intense Experiences do not present themselves, but instead that people don't take notice of them and don't let these positive Intense Experiences work their magic. People are certainly not actively and routinely bringing these positive Intense Experiences into their lives, which is precisely what this book invites you to do.

Instead, people are largely suffering from Muddy Slope Syndrome. They feel as if they're far off the path of attaining their biggest goals, dreams, passions, and intentions. Many feel stuck in dead-end jobs or in unsatisfying relationships that, more often than not, really can be improved. People feel exhausted, mired in mediocre lives, as if they never have enough time, and they're wondering, Is this all there is?

When asked, many people will say, "Yes, I am okay, life is pretty good." Putting that face on for the world is the thing to do. But

I would bet my house that everyone reading this right now can identify when I say that deep down inside, in those quiet moments, perhaps when you are alone with yourself and don't have to smile and pose for your job and the world, the truth often surfaces: there are many things you know you are meant to achieve, become, and experience in this life, but it just feels like one barrier after another prevents you from achieving them.

As the author George Eliot noted, however, "It is never too late to be what you might have been." You don't need to depend on surviving tragedies to keep refocusing yourself on what matters most, on living the life of your dreams. You don't need to rely on making it through difficult challenges to get off the muddy slope and regain your focus on achieving the success you are meant to achieve.

Remarkably successful and happy people stay focused on positive Intense Experiences, particularly within nine key areas, to keep them off that muddy slope and instead on their path to achieving their greatest goals, as well as deep inner peace and happiness. You absolutely can, too. With the book you hold in your hand, you will.

You will quickly start making powerful self-discoveries and clearing the path to your greatest happiness and success by delving into just one of the Intense Experiences. Instead of feeling like you have even more to work to do, you will actually *enjoy* the exercises in the 9 Intense Experiences that enable each experience to work its magic back on you. You will bust through the self-sabotaging rust and crust that have accrued from emotions such as stress, fear, guilt, anger, depression, worry, and feeling overwhelmed.

You are no less deserving than those who, by staying committed to Intense Experiences, achieved the success and happiness they knew they were meant to. With the book you hold in your hands, you will achieve what you know deep inside you are meant to—in your finances, career, relationships, health, and other key areas of life. You will discover what a beautiful thing it is, this becoming who you already know you are.

Which of These Two Types Are You?

To effectively and enjoyably experience part II, it is beneficial to know if you consider yourself

1. A more rational, organizational, and analytical left-brain person
2. A more experiential, intuitive, and holistic right-brain person

Left-brainers often enjoy math and numbers, have orderly filing systems and neat workspaces, tend to be good at keeping appointments, listen to *what* is being said, prefer to work up to the whole, step by step, and tend to be engineers, electricians, and accountants. Right-brainers are often engaged in the arts, have cluttered or seemingly disordered workspaces, tend to be late and consider it no big deal, listen to *how* things are being said, want to see the whole first and then dig into the details, and tend to be entrepreneurs, musicians, and salespeople.

If you are more left-brained, you will likely gain the most benefit by reading the first Intense Experience and doing the exercises within it before moving on to the second experience and so on.

If you are more right-brained, you will probably benefit most by reading the entire book, to see how the nine experiences are interconnected and will create a powerful overall transformation, even as you begin to delve into the exercises in the first experience, then continue to those in the second experience, and so on.

I strongly recommend that you complete the exercises within one experience before moving on to the next. If you immerse yourself in the exercises in one area over a week or two, this adds to the self-revealing "magic" that you may miss if you repeatedly leapfrog to exercises across different experiences. If you are drawn to jump over to other exercises, however, that is far more beneficial than not doing them at all!

Although you will gain maximum benefit from doing all of the exercises within each experience—you'll be surprised at what is revealed to you by even those you aren't sure about doing—if there are any that you absolutely don't want to do, fine. Don't do them. You'll still experience amazing insights and transformation from the exercises that you do.

Turn off the Poison Valves

I cannot stress this enough: while engaging in these Intense Experiences and ideally for the rest of your life, turn off the poison valves.

Doing so is a mighty Intense Experience unto itself. It will also help drive the self-revelations and the positive transformations in store for you much more deeply and rapidly.

The poison valves are those experiences you allow into your being that leave you feeling stressed out, worried, angry, and down. They often include certain TV or radio programs that call themselves the news but are actually the *bad* news, which focus on stories of deception, hate, murder, rape, and greed. These topics may result in good ratings, but they make it hard for you not to believe the whole world sucks. Still, every single day the sun rises, babies laugh, puppies are born, opportunities are endless, you continue to be alive, in fact almost no one dies, and the news goes unreported of a million times more good deeds and experiences than there are bad deeds and experiences. The poison valves often include certain highly judgmental and negative talk shows that tear people down, versus fairly discussing and challenging ideas. The poison valves may include individuals in your life who also do these things or who otherwise suck the energy, potential, and joy right out of you.

Even before part II begins, here is an important exercise for you to try: carefully consider all of the poison valves to which you routinely expose yourself. Think of the TV and radio shows, the Web sites, the print publications, the people, the places, the types of music, and even the kinds of food you routinely consume. How do you really feel while taking them in and afterward?

People are often surprised to discover that certain things they normally expose themselves to are toxic to their minds, hearts, bodies, and spirits. Isolate the potential toxins, and shut off those poison valves. To experience how powerful and positive this is, try it for even a week or two, as you delve into the exercises in the first Intense Experience. Don't watch or listen to the TV programs and don't read the publications on your poison list. As for the people, if they are individuals you cannot avoid, at least turn their poison valves down. Practice selective listening: separate the actions you are required to perform for them out of love, duty, or a paycheck from the toxic words and expressions that ooze from them. Tune out this negativity. Smile a lot, and be really kind to them.

Turning off the poison valves is like deciding to go on a healthy diet and eliminating all of the junk food from your pantry and refrigerator and getting rid of all of the fast-food restaurants and doughnut shops within a fifty-four mile radius of your home, too.

Before Each Exercise, Prime Your Hippocampus

Your hippocampus is located in the middle-lower portion of your brain. It is instrumental in turning new information and experiences into long-term "memories" that the rest of your brain and your being can use to permanently change and improve you.

The reason you may remember one exquisite meal you ate on a certain day five years ago but you can't remember the other two meals you ate that day is in large part that your hippocampus was primed by your riveted attention to the delicious gourmet experience.

To really let the exercises within each experience permanently work their "magic" on you, it is highly recommended that you prime yourself for the exercise by clearing your head of other stuff and giving each exercise your full attention. No multitasking here, this is too important.

If you practice prayer, meditation, deep breathing, yoga, or stretching, it can be quite beneficial to calm and center yourself with these practices prior to delving into each exercise.

Write in Your Journal Afterward

One more strong recommendation: after each exercise, jot down your responses to it in a journal. Write about what the exercise has revealed to you regarding your emotions and thought processes, your relationships with other people, your goals, barriers it has helped you break through, what you now see more clearly, and whatever else comes to mind.

The benefits of writing down your responses to the experiences have been well documented; for example, it is a powerful way to transfer the experience to your hippocampus so that its benefits become a permanent part of your being. It is also useful and enjoyable to go back months or years later and read your journals.

You can do this journaling in many ways, of course: on your computer, on cocktail napkins, and so on. But since you're worth it, consider getting a bound notebook with blank pages and recording your impressions there. This is a little Intense Experience in itself, because choosing the right journal, the right cover and type of paper, and then taking the time to write your impressions by hand, is an act of honoring yourself and your worth.

Yet even if you choose blank pieces of paper, or you record your responses via audio or video, the act of journaling after each exercise enhances your self-awareness and the powerful and inevitable changes you will experience.

Part II

✺

The 9 Intense Experiences

A mind that is stretched by a new experience can never go back to its old dimensions.

—Oliver Wendell Holmes

I hear and I forget. I see and I remember. I do and I understand.

—Chinese proverb

Don't ask what the world needs. Ask what makes you come alive, and go do it. Because what the world needs is people who have come alive.

—Howard Thurman

Intense Experience #1

෨

Journey Back to Neverland

We don't stop playing because we grow old; we grow old because we stop playing.

—George Bernard Shaw

You can't depend on your eyes when your imagination is out of focus.

—Mark Twain

Play is the exultation of the possible.

—Martin Buber

What if you could go to a place, whenever you chose, that restored your sense of wonder with the world, in your relationships, and with yourself? That sparked your creativity and energy? That made you feel as alive as a child immersed in play and as if you had all the time you need in the world?

You can. It's easy and fun.

But let's first go to the chilly opposite of this place, to the mind-set that most adults have trapped themselves in today. This mind-set displays itself in countless ways, but perhaps none more apparent than in the most common answer to a typical question. See if this sounds familiar.

"Hi, how are you?" Jennifer asks.

"I'm good, but I'm just so busy!" Gina responds.

Jennifer knowingly nods and adds, "I know what you mean—there is just never enough time in the day!" Or some slight variation thereof.

This conversation, like an old log you walk right by every day, is rather strange when you slow down and really examine it. By exclaiming how busy they are, by repeating for the zillionth time how they never have enough time, people aren't merely stating how they feel; they're seeking instant understanding and acceptance from others. And because Muddy Slope Syndrome is so widespread, they always get that instant understanding and acceptance. These strange mantras are in fact worn and displayed like merit badges.

"Oh, you're overwhelmed and feel drained of your energy and have too much to do, too?" people might as well say. "And you don't feel like you even have time to breathe? Well, good, you are normal. Join the club! You are suffering and dysfunctional along with the rest of us!"

By repeating the mantra constantly, even in a seemingly innocent conversation like this, people are also engraining deep into themselves the belief that they're so busy and simply don't have time—for what really matters, for their biggest dreams, for profound love and happiness.

Because this dysfunctional mind-set is so prevalent, here's something you may not immediately believe: you are given all of the time you need. Your grandparents, their grandparents, and your ancient ancestors all had the same amount of time in a day (but not nearly as much time as you do over a lifetime).

A day is still a day. An hour is still an hour. What has changed instead are people's values and therefore their perspective. Although many people will claim to value their big goals and dreams, their relaxation and playtime, their actions are severely out of sync with their words. As the Harvard economist Juliet

Schor portrayed in her classic book *The Overworked American*, and as the recent global economic crash so ruthlessly confirmed, what people's actions indicate that they value highly is consuming stuff—and working their butts off to get it. Marketers are paid big bucks and have thousands of psychological tactics available to them to make people believe that this stuff will improve their lives and make them happier. Whether they work in the business world, in academia, or as homemakers, people get trapped into working to utter exhaustion in order to pay for all of the empty promises and to try to take care of their stuff.

Since the 1950s, for example, the living area per family in new single-family houses built in the United States has increased by a factor of three. Yet although people have been sold into believing that bigger homes mean they'll be as happy as a (fictional) king or celebrity and that all of that extra space will surely equal more comfort, there are no correlations between a larger home and greater happiness. Instead, as Sonja Lyubomirsky, the University of California–Riverside professor of psychology and author of *The How of Happiness*, noted, "Someone who feels elated after upgrading to a big house is likely to soon start yearning for more—an extra bedroom, a pool, whatever it may be." As a 2009 Wharton School of Business study found, home ownership itself doesn't even lead to happiness. The study found no link between home ownership and self-esteem and no difference in stress levels between homeowners and renters; it also proved that homeowners actually spent less time in active leisure pursuits than renters did and 4 to 6 percent less time interacting with friends and neighbors.

What all of that extra space in bigger houses then requires is for people to buy more stuff to fill the space and taking care of it. Which means spending more money, which results in people working more to make that money. Or, more likely, going deeper into debt. Furthermore, because parents demonstrate such allegiance to working themselves to death to make money to pay for their ever-growing debt from buying more stuff (which merely suffocates their energy and their dreams), then children are pushed more deeply into this same deadly mind trap. Children learn what they live, and the overwhelmed child—with school, homework, after-school and weekend lessons, college entrance exams, the need to get a great job, pressure!—has become a sad cliché. Here's another mind-blowing fact: according to a University of Michigan study, children have lost twelve hours per week of free time since the 1970s!

In whatever "free" time they do have, children today usually have their eyes buried in one screen or another: the TV screen, the computer screen, the cell phone screen, or the video game screen. Here, too, though, children are only learning from and having their habits reinforced by adults. According to a 2009 study published in the *New York Times*, adults have TV, computer, cell phone, GPS, and other screens in their faces an astonishing 8.5 hours per day.

A Flamingo with Lagoons Flying over It

People's actions do not align with their stated beliefs about what really matters in life. Overwork is rampant because people are pursuing money to buy more deceptive stuff or to pay off the debt from doing so. Their ever-shrinking "free time" is spent not on enlivening and transformative experiences but on vegetative to deadly pursuits, such as (mostly bad) TV and shopping. There is little wonder that people feel overwhelmed, stressed out, depressed, drained of energy, and jaded.

A much-touted study, reported on CNN and elsewhere early in 2009, discovered what anyone can realize through common sense (when he or she slows down enough to consider it): experiences make us happier than material purchases do. People feel a greater sense of "being alive" through experiences. They feel more happiness and satisfaction not only immediately after the experience, but also well down the line (versus that immediate "high" they may get from a material purchase such as a pair of new jeans, which quickly wears off and leaves them seeking their next fix). According to Ryan T. Howell, an assistant professor of psychology at San Francisco State University and author of the study, experiential purchases resulted in a greater sense of energy, purpose, and social connectedness. Money actually can help buy happiness when it is spent on rewarding experiences, such as comedy shows, dance lessons, nature expeditions, or art classes.

What are you putting into your being? Which experiences do you engage in that are good for you, and which are detrimental to your health, happiness, energy levels—and even your perception of time? And how often do you partake in one of the most important experiences of all: journeying back to Neverland?

In *Peter Pan*, Neverland is the island home of Peter Pan, Tinker Bell, the Lost Boys, mermaids, pirates, and other assorted colorful characters. The place has no boundaries, and even its geography varies according to whose heart and eyes perceive it: for example, in the eyes of the character John, it "had a lagoon with flamingoes flying over it," while in the eyes of his brother Michael, it "had a flamingo with lagoons flying over it."

In a metaphorical sense, Neverland stands for boundless imagination, creativity, freedom, and—a key word here—timelessness. Yet in excess, it also stands for escapism and selfishness. Neverland is a great and important place to routinely visit, but you wouldn't want to live there.

On the contrary, because people work longer hours, fill their "free time" with still more tasks from their seemingly endless to-do lists, spend less time in leisure pursuits, and—here's the kicker—feel guilty when they don't get something checked off that endless to-do list, today virtually all grown-ups are suffering from an extreme lack of journeying back to Neverland.

Virtually every adult is not letting his or her mind, heart, body, and spirit play enough. This warps our perception of time and what truly matters in life. It crushes our sense of feeling boundless, hopeful, and free and therefore crushes our potential. It deflates energy and creativity, and thus decreases our productivity. I could go on, but to sum it up, it really sucks.

Reagan Whittles, Eisenhower Putts, and Kennedy Canters

Contemporary society may marginalize adult play as something that is frivolous—nice, if you can do it, but a distant second in importance to work. And many adults may feel guilty about playing and not "getting something more important" done.

Yet from Plato and Aristotle down to Sartre and Homer Simpson, philosophers have noted the centrality of play to promote human health and happiness. Play is also highly respected in many religions. To many Christians and Jews, the seventh day of the week, the Sabbath, is a day to praise God, relax, and bond with family and friends and to play—to take recreation (re-creation!)—out in nature among God's miracles. In various Christian denominations and other religions, forms of jubilant play such as singing out and dancing are also essential ways to worship God.

Meanwhile, leading contemporary psychological researchers such as Martin Seligman and Lenore Terr have noted that the three pillars of mental health are love, work, and play. Many recent studies have demonstrated the importance of various forms of play to adult health and happiness. For example, participating in various forms of mental play, such as board games, quilting, or making pottery, can prevent memory loss as you grow older. Social dancing can ward off illness and counteract physical and mental declines due to aging. Listening to children's music can open adults' minds and make them more empathetic. Reading for pleasure, in addition to its many intellectual benefits, such as improved language skills, can dramatically enhance empathetic skills and decision-making abilities. A nine-year study of more than twelve thousand men found that annual vacations significantly reduce the risk of death for middle-age men, while a twenty-year study of women by the

Centers for Disease Control found a strong correlation between a higher risk of heart attack and death and a lack of vacations.

Even with some of the world's most endless to-do lists, U.S. presidents have understood the extreme importance of frequently journeying back to Neverland. For more than fifty years, Camp David, tucked away in Maryland's Catoctin Mountains, has been the official presidential retreat. Gerald Ford loved snowmobiling there, John F. Kennedy went horseback riding there, and Ronald Reagan enjoyed using the Camp David woodworking shop. At the White House, Theodore Roosevelt first had tennis courts installed in 1909. Dwight Eisenhower created a putting green with a sand trap there during his term. President Nixon constructed a bowling alley. The senior George Bush put in horseshoe pits and a basketball court. Bill Clinton added a practice green. And Barack Obama had court lines painted and removable nets installed on the basketball court.

In fact, according to the Pulitzer Prize–winning historian Doris Kearns Goodwin, a firm commitment to relaxation and leisure activity despite their heavy workload—or really in order to best perform at that work—is one of the ten qualities that make for the most effective presidents. Franklin D. Roosevelt had a nightly cocktail hour in which guests told funny stories and enjoyed themselves—and never spoke of politics. Abraham Lincoln was renowned for his humor and telling long stories that enabled him to "whistle off sadness."

Great philosophers have argued it. U.S. presidents have lived it. Scientific research keeps confirming it. And I've seen it repeatedly with people who have gone through the exercises that follow: letting your mind, heart, body, and spirit play is a seemingly miraculous way to increase your energy, shake off self-sabotaging emotions like depression and fear, boost your creativity and clarity, and reveal to yourself, or refocus yourself on, whatever truly matters most to you.

In a world where the power of play is disrespected, where you're provoked to feel guilty about playing but encouraged to brag about how busy you are, it is easy to lose sight of the extreme importance of this experience.

I hope that by now this idea simply feels like common sense. Maybe you recall how you felt during and after any recent play-time you have allowed yourself as an adult, be it singing out loud in the car, taking an unrushed vacation, building a sandcastle, or scrapbooking.

The widespread perception is that life is hard and so busy, and there's not enough time for anything. People think that play is only a secondary activity, something to squeeze in here or there if they have the time, and something to feel guilty about if they do it when they've got "more important" things to do. The joy, clarity, creativity, love, timelessness, and inner peace that arise from play are widely perceived to be the exceptions in a predominantly busy, overwhelming, stressful world.

These perceptions of life being hard and not having enough time are ridiculous and quite self-abusive. On an individual level they grind down our happiness, our zest for life, and our potential. On a mass level, they grind down our collective happiness and our drive and potential to create solutions to war, disease, environmental issues, and much more. What is the aim of life if not to experience that which promotes joy, energy, love, creativity, clarity, and motivation, as a rule, and in the process to cast aside dysfunctional beliefs about life? We were not put on earth to waste our lives on endless work in order to buy more stuff that never delivers on its promises.

As Stuart Brown, the author of the exceptional book *Play: How It Shapes the Brain, Opens the Imagination, and Reinvigorates the Soul*, noted, "When we engage in fantasy play at any age, we bend the reality of our ordinary lives, and in the process germinate new ideas and new ways of being."

Although stories, studies, and statistics may motivate and add credence for you, the whole point of Intense Experiences is that you will discover remarkable benefits and inevitable changes only by *doing.* Let go of any notion that the following exercises are silly, that you're too old and busy now and have more important things to do, that life is meant to hurt, and that Trix are for kids. If you have a hard time letting go of these notions, engage in the first exercise extra vigorously. Leap right into these exercises to Journey Back to Neverland, and prepare to be amazed.

Five Intense Questions for You

1. Bowling, yodeling, dancing, backgammon, boating, gardening, quilting, Jello wrestling—in what ways do you already frequently "Journey Back to Neverland" as an adult?

2. Various methods of playing can produce different benefits— for example, by sparking your creativity and energy, calming and centering you, or improving your memory. How do you tend to feel after each of the different ways you already typically play?

3. What types of barriers may prevent you from playing more? Guilt? Feeling uncertain that play is worthwhile and what a responsible adult "should" be doing, given all of your other priorities?

4. Do you believe it would benefit you in terms of your overall happiness, inner peace, and success at achieving your goals to Journey Back to Neverland more often? And to expand your play experiences into new areas that can produce new self-revelations and benefits? (If yes, please immerse yourself in the exercises that follow! If no, please definitely immerse yourself in the exercises that follow!)

5. Around the ages of six to nine, one of my favorite playtime activities was to lock my bedroom door and imagine that I was Alice Cooper, although I recall seeing the hard rock legend, in his painted-on scary face and long straggly black hair, only once on TV. Still, I was Alice Cooper. I'd leap around on the bed, wailing the only lyrics I knew by

him—"School's out for summer! School's out for-ever!"—
into my toilet-paper-tube microphone to my audience of
stuffed animals. That certainly suggests something about
my character and love of the stage, and one of these days,
in a live interview or a seminar, I'm sure I won't be able to
resist breaking out into my Alice Cooper routine. With that
to inspire you . . .

What were your favorite ways of playing as a child? Can
you see parallels in how this helped make you who you are
today, in terms of your character, relationships, career, and likes
and dislikes?

The Journey Back to Neverland Exercises

Exercise 1: Bust It Open!

That's how the rapper T.I. puts it: Bust it open! Not being a
rapper, except in the shower, here's how I'll put it: Dance.

Shake, twist, rattle, and roll your body freely to your favorite
music to physically start breaking up that emotional rust and crust
that has accumulated on your heart and spirit over the years and
the decades. Everyone has at least a little rust and crust, and most
adults have a lot.

It doesn't matter if you haven't danced for years; if you're
a Fortune 500 CEO, a priest, a great-grandma, a Nobel Prize–
winning physicist; if you have use of only part of your body; or all
of these. And while dancing with others has some added benefits,
such as enhancing bonds and feelings of belonging and not being
the only one who looks silly trying out new moves, if you are only
willing to do it alone behind your locked and barricaded bedroom
door, so-help-you-God, that's fine.

Just dance. At least for the next week or two, while you
immerse yourself in these Journey Back to Neverland exercises,

dance often, even if it's just a little shimmy and shake here and a little heel-toe, heel-toe, slide slide slide there.

Alternately, if it's more your thing, get yourself some drums—a cheap snare drum, a tambourine, maracas, and bongos from the toy store work just fine—and bang away often.

Even better, and regardless of whether you'd be one of the jokes on *American Idol*, sing out as often as you can while you dance or drum.

As Stuart Brown, the author of *Play* and founder of the National Institute for Play, noted, "Movement lights up the brain and fosters learning, innovation, flexibility, adaptability and resilience."

There's an important reason why this simple exercise comes first in this experience and this book. Most adults nowadays are trapped in more mind-, body-, and spirit-numbing routines than they are aware of. Whether you are an office worker, a homemaker, a service worker, or a laborer or you do virtually any type of work, if you could somehow attach diodes to your body and then watch a graphic replay of the course of your movements during a given week, you'd likely notice that your movements are largely repetitive and quite limited, given the range of their potential.

Most people—in body, mind, and spirit—are suffering from repetitive stress syndrome of a different sort and on a grand scale. This act of dancing freely, banging on the drums wildly, and singing out loud will break through the physical repetition your body is caught in.

Perhaps we all should have been born with labels on our bellies that read "Shake Well before Use." Because when we get trapped in physical, mental, and emotional routines, that rust and crust residue tends to clog us up, and all of our best stuff tends to settle somewhere deep inside us, where it's not immediately available. Dancing with abandon or banging away on drums shakes off that constricting residue, and gets our creativity, memory, clarity, motivation, and our other best stuff flowing to the top again.

Shake well, and shake often.

Exercise 2: Get the Rust Out

Over the next week or two, indulge in plenty of pixie dust: not some illegal powdered drug, but the "Best of Neverland" media. This includes movies, music, literature, and more, all of which, though suitable for children ages eight and up, are really magical and transformative experiences for adults, too.

You'll discover that by replacing what you typically watch, read, or listen to with Neverland masterpieces, a lot more will take place inside you than your simply being entertained. Just as dancing and drumming shake your body loose, experiencing these stories and messages is a powerful way to shake that rust and crust—caked on from years or decades of Muddy Slope Syndrome—loose from your heart and mind.

A special note for parents and grandparents of young kids: although you've likely experienced some of these Neverland classics with your kids and you might in fact live half of your life with a Disney or Pixar movie playing in the background, I strongly encourage you to experience these *alone*. Immersing yourself in these art forms *for* yourself, when you can actually focus entirely on them, is a vastly different experience that will provide powerful insights into yourself and more.

Following are some strong recommendations for Journey Back to Neverland books and movies. If there are other books, movies, and so on, that call to you instead—perhaps those you loved when you were younger, or those recommended by someone you trust—by all means yes, listen to their call!

Books

Alice's Adventures in Wonderland, Lewis Carroll. From the Mad Hatter to the Cheshire Cat to the Queen of Hearts, this book and all of its glorious eccentricities will open doors to wonderful places inside you that you didn't even know existed—places that can transform how you view your world.

The Little Prince, **Antoine de Saint Exupéry.** Definitely read this one! A stranded pilot encounters a little prince and shares who and what he has encountered on his journeys. The Little Prince, wise in the way a child can be, discovers what is truly important—and you will rediscover as much, too.

Peter Pan, **J. M. Barrie.** This is the ultimate children's story that kids up to age 106 should read again and again throughout their lives. Why? Other than the kind-of-slow introductory chapter, it's an enchanting story written so delightfully by J. M. Barrie that you'll sometimes find yourself rereading a passage just for its wonderfulness, and you'll chuckle aloud frequently.

Movies

E.T. This movie about a lost alien and a young boy quite simply *is* love and imagination incarnate.

Fantasia. Back in the late 1930s, Disney animators set out to interpret classical music on the screen, and this masterpiece is the result.

Other Neverland Reads You'll Love

Charlotte's Web, E. B. White

A Christmas Carol, Charles Dickens

The Chronicles of Narnia, C. S. Lewis

The Giving Tree, Shel Silverstein

The Harry Potter books, J. K. Rowling

James and the Giant Peach, Roald Dahl

The Phantom Tollbooth, Norman Justin

Pinocchio, Carlo Collodi

The Velveteen Rabbit, Margery Williams

Winnie-the-Pooh, A. A. Milne

Finding Nemo. Whether you're six or eighty-six, you're going to be awed and inspired by this Pixar masterpiece that takes you into Nemo's underwater world in Australia's Great Barrier Reef.

The Iron Giant. A gorgeously animated story of a massive metal-eating robot from another world and the boy who, despite the grown-ups' fear of the robot, befriends him. For how powerfully and delicately it serves its message of what love truly is and what really matters in life, this is my all-time favorite children's movie and ideal for your Journey to Neverland experience.

Spirited Away. This may be unlike any animated movie you've ever experienced. It is the highest-grossing film of all time in Japan for good reason, because it will leave you exploring the very nature of your own identity.

The Wizard of Oz. Perhaps you've experienced the magic of Dorothy and her little dog, too, fifty-four times, but it's definitely worth seeing again.

As for music, what works best for this experience is to dive back into the music you loved during those magical years when you were around eight to twelve years old. Music has its own unique and powerful ability to penetrate through all of that rust and crust. Unless those years were very difficult for you and you don't fondly recall any music from that period, you'll find that surrounding yourself with those songs once again can quickly restore the wonder, excitement, and boundless joy you felt when you used to listen to them. The *Grease* soundtrack? *The Sound of Music, Dirty Dancing,* or *Footloose?* Sean Cassidy, Journey, the Beatles? Consider the music you loved back then, and get the CD or download it for this experience!

Other Neverland Movies You'll Love:

Aladdin

Babe

Beauty and the Beast

Big

Big Fish

Edward Scissorhands

Goonies

The Harry Potter movies

Howl's Moving Castle

The Incredibles

It's a Wonderful Life

The Lion King

The Little Mermaid

The Lord of the Rings trilogy

Mary Poppins

Mrs. Doubtfire

The Muppet Movie

My Neighbor Totoro

The Neverending Story

The Nightmare before Christmas

The Pirates of the Caribbean

The Princess Bride

Ratatouille

The Red Balloon

The Secret Garden

Shrek

The Snowman

Snow White and the Seven Dwarfs

The Sound of Music

The Star Wars movies

Toy Story

Up!

Wallace & Gromit

Wall-E

Whale Rider

Who Framed Roger Rabbit?

Willy Wonka and the Chocolate Factory

Exercise 3: Pull a Ferris Bueller's Day Off

In the 1986 movie *Ferris Bueller's Day Off*, Ferris fakes an illness, takes the day off from school with a couple of friends, and has the time of his life, learning a number of important lessons along the way.

During the two or three weeks you immerse yourself in this experience, pull a Ferris! Take at least one day off from the routine of your life. This doesn't necessarily mean calling in sick from work or school. Many people jam their weekend with chores and errands and end up having no weekend at all, so consider playing hooky from that. At the least, plan a number of extended recesses during which you genuinely play and don't do anything because you *have* to do it.

You'll discover that this is actually one of the most important things you can do in life, and that you're likely not doing it enough. By doing it now, and experiencing what it does for you, you will be reminding your spirit, your deepest self, of where your priorities reside.

"No, my lovely and very cool spirit," you will say via this exercise, "although I may have slipped into a rut where it seemed like

I valued work and errands and maybe TV, too, as top priorities in my life, the truth is, having fun and really living life like this is just as, if not more, important. I know I'm not here to suffer."

Here are some recommendations for Back to Neverland things to do when you play hooky or take recess:

- Go to a water park, a carnival, or an amusement park. Give yourself permission to have some cotton candy or funnel cake while you're there! You can cancel out its effects with broccoli and green tea later.
- Go mini-golfing, paintballing, go-carting, or laser-tagging.
- Go to a neighborhood playground. Ride the swings, build something in the sandbox. If you're a man, however, bring a kid or a female friend so that no one, um, wonders.
- Go to see a new children's movie on the big screen at a theater. Get the popcorn and the licorice.
- Go to see a children's play. This could mean a professional theater production of a play geared toward children or a school production where kids are in the play.
- Go to a museum, especially one that has fun interactive displays.
- Grab a few friends and go toilet-paper your favorite neighbor's house and trees. Just kidding! Don't do this, and don't say I suggested it if you do!

Exercise 4: Go Low and Play

How often do you spend some quality time down on the floor or, even better, down on the lawn or the ground? Searching for your lost contact lens, installing tile, or cleaning up dog pee does not count as quality time. Unless you're a passionate gardener, or perhaps if you have a toddler or a cuddly pet, you likely don't go low nearly enough.

Think of how and where you typically spend your life. During the night, you're on your back, side, or stomach on a bed or a couch. During the day, if you're like almost everyone else, you're sitting in some type of seat—a lot of sitting—and you're also upright whenever you either move or stand still.

Yet as photographers, painters, graphic artists, and architects well know, altering your literal perspective can help alter your conscious perspective on your issues, goals, and life in general.

To discover this on your own, during the course of this experience get down as often as possible where you used to spend more time in your youth: on the floor. As you will discover in the Wander into the Forest Intense Experience, adults are dangerously deficient in physical contact with natural surfaces, so it is even better if you can get down on the lawn, the soil, or the sand. While you're down there, quadruple the transformative power of this exercise by playing with your favorite childhood toys.

I know I railed against overconsumption earlier, but some shopping is necessary. And this definitely qualifies. Consider the two or three more creative-oriented toys that you absolutely loved when you were around eight to eleven years old—or those your friends had and you wished you had—and buy them. (Unless you know a kid who has them; you can borrow them or try to offer your wisdom in exchange.) Etch-a-Sketch or Lite Brite? Play-Doh? LEGO bricks or Lincoln Logs? The big box of Crayola crayons and paper? Dominoes, jigsaw puzzles, or marbles?

Whatever your favorites may be, shut off your cell phone; forget your e-mail; if you have kids, let them play alongside you (remember to share!); and get down on the floor or the ground outside and engage in some creative play. Start assembling a puzzle, and over the next couple of weeks finish it. Build your dream home out of LEGO bricks or sand or a combination of both. Use crayons or markers to draw and color a scene or two from the dream you had last night. Sign it and stick it on your refrigerator when you're done. Build your ex-lover or ex-spouse out of

Play-Doh, exaggerating or minimizing certain bodily features—and then take the figure in your hand and smash it! Or create something a bit nicer.

Get down and engage in some creative play, and do it often. I again urge you to start, during this experience, with the favorite toys from your youth because this can quickly open some long-closed doors. The main idea in this book is for you to embrace these experiences permanently in your life, so down the line you can switch to more adult-oriented playing, such as scrapbooking or building model cars. But if you discover that you still absolutely love those Shrinky Dinks, then stick with them!

This exercise will give you a new perspective. It will open your heart and mind and soothe your spirit. You'll be quite surprised at what this exercise alone will do for you in terms of providing far greater clarity, creativity, energy, patience, and resolve to help you see and achieve your life's goals and solve problems at home and at work.

Exercise 5: What's Your Story?

Stories are *how* we connect to one another. They are how we identify. In any conversation, you are sharing a story or a piece of one. All marketing and advertising tell a story—the story of how you will improve and be happier if you buy a certain product. Religion is about the sharing of stories and attempting to deliver, find, and hold onto faith through those stories. When you head off on a vacation, you're anticipating a story, and when you return, you have a story—usually a different one from what you anticipated. Even job interviews are a story: this is the story of what I know, how I am, what I will do in the job, and therefore why I am the ideal candidate.

Overwhelmingly, though, the stories that adults hear from the outside world are negative. Gloom-and-doom stories in the news. Stories spread by rampant marketing and advertising of how this thing and that stuff will make us better, faster, and stronger—stories that are almost always untrue and deflating. Derogatory stories of how insane this music star is and what a jerk that baseball player is.

Overwhelmingly, the stories that adults tell one another are negative. How overly busy they are. How they never have time for anything. How this person or that person sucks. How prices suck, politicians suck, work sucks, and life sucks.

Yet the world—and your world—is overflowing with good stories. Stories that need to be told. Recalling your own best stories has a powerful cathartic effect. Sharing those stories and hearing others' good stories are even more powerful ways to purge the rust and the crust—the stress, fear, sadness, and apathy—from your head, heart, and spirit.

For the next week or two, at least, and hopefully for the rest of your life, try to recall your best stories. Share them with others, and ask them for their best stories, too.

Whether you do it while taking a walk, while performing a rote chore, or while sitting on the toilet or driving, ask yourself,

- What have been the most inspiring episodes in my life that are worth remembering and telling others?
- What are the funniest events in my life that are worth remembering and retelling?
- Even with the challenging and tragic events I have experienced in life, what has been their silver lining? How have I, or how can I, better myself via the lessons they have provided? When I am telling these tragic stories to others, what true happy ending will I give them?

Share your good stories with family and friends at meals, during work, and on the train. It will help them, too. And ask them for their good stories—their most inspiring, happiest, most cathartic tales. Everyone has many stories worth sharing.

Finally, write down your good stories in your journal. Or record them and post them on YouTube for your family and friends, and for the world, to see—we always need more good stories. Most of all, write or record these good stories so that you can revisit them yourself when you feel down, anxious, overwhelmed, lonely, or apathetic. This way, you can remind yourself that life is full of goodness and potential and that even the thunderstorm periods in your life will bring flowers.

Years down the line, you will treasure these stories. Someday your children, grandchildren, siblings, friends, and others may treasure and need these stories, too. I am sure you realize now, and will even more so in the future, that remembering and sharing these stories is far more important than any e-mail you could be answering or any carpet you could be vacuuming.

Exercise 6: Add Pep to the Grind

When I wash the dishes, it may appear to others as if I am simply washing the dishes, but I am never just washing the dishes.

Sometimes instead I am a Roman dishwashing slave, and as I scrub and rinse this time, I am actually planning my escape. The master will walk by in five minutes, so I save the big pot, the beer mug, and the knives on the "dirty dishes side" of the sink for that moment. When the master walks by, I will smack him with the pot, then the mug, then grab the knives for protection and run out of the house and all the way back to my homeland. In my mind, I always make it.

Other times, I am in a dishwashing race; to date, I am undefeated. Occasionally, I am in a spot-free dishes contest; this one I have yet to win. These days, I always find a way to turn dishwashing into play—so much so, that I often don't use my automatic dishwasher.

It is the same with many other tasks in my life that I used to consider boring or irritating. During long business meetings, I've been known to make funny faces at others across the table. Sometimes these escalate into an all-out battle of funny faces among those present. Some people may argue that this frivolity prevents business from being accomplished; I'd counterargue that it actually increases productivity by bringing the dead back to life, opening hearts and minds, and improving morale and bonding. Those of you who would criticize it, especially if you're considered the "serious" type, should instead try it: stick your tongue out and cross your eyes at someone during your next meeting.

When you think of fun in general, chances are you don't think of sitting in meetings, washing the dishes, paying your bills, cleaning out the cat litter, or being stuck in a traffic jam. You probably consider such tasks mundane or frustrating.

Yet if you bring a sense of play to these things, your mind-set, mood, and energy levels will change. At first glance, bringing this sense of play to the "chores" in your life may seem minor, but when you add up how many of these tasks exist in your life, you can see how the change could be huge.

For this exercise, it really pays for you to make a list of all of the tasks in your life that currently bore or irritate you—those you'd love to put off or cancel altogether. Then determine how you can transform those tasks into something more enjoyable and perhaps even meaningful.

If you're often stuck in traffic, be sure to listen to funny recordings of comedians or music you can sing along to, and also take a look at the other drivers around you. Imagine—from the expressions on their faces, how they're dressed—what they do for a living, what their relationships are like, how they'd be in bed—whatever entertains you. (This makes for more compassionate driving, too!)

If you work in a service job, such as a cashier in a grocery store or a coffee shop, make it more fun by asking customers ridiculous questions. "Would you like to add a box of cornstarch to your order today?" or "Would you like your coffee in a cup today?"

When you ride the elevator, play I Spy with other people on the elevator. It will brighten their ride and their day, too.

Whether you create internal stories, such as my Roman dishwashing slave tale, or you perform external actions—if you work in a cubicle farm, try starting the wave as fans do at sporting events—there is always a way to transform the mundane and irritating into something more enjoyable. Certain tasks take more practice than others, but you'll be surprised at what a big change this can make in your life.

Exercise 7: Throw Tomatoes

On the last Wednesday of August in the town of Bunol, Spain, between twenty and fifty thousand people, most clad in T-shirts, shorts, and goggles, gather for La Tomatina. The origins of this increasingly popular event are unclear; some believe it began as a food fight among friends, others as a practical joke on a bad musician. Nearly 140 tons of tomatoes are trucked into the center of town for the festival. When the water cannon blows, the chaos begins. For one hour, participants grab the tomatoes, squish them in their hands to get them juicy, and run through the streets throwing them at one another. The media and their cameras are also favorite tomato targets. There are no winners or losers in this war, and the only aim is to have all-out fun. Afterward, the streets flow with tomato juice and slush, until the city washes it away.

Some people might wonder, Why waste all of those tomatoes, why attend an event like this at all? For the sheer transformational joy of it, I wonder why anyone *wouldn't* want to attend.

I'm not insisting you organize a mass tomato war. But I am urging you to gather adult friends, family, work mates, and anyone you choose—three or more people makes a party!—for some type of playful event that you do simply for the sheer transformational joy of it.

A hot dog battle, to include ketchup, mustard, relish, and other toppings, if you have access to a field where the foods can become nutrients for the soil? A whipped-cream pie fight like the one in that *Brady Bunch* episode? A water balloon fight, a snowball fight, or a feather pillow fight? Before you discount these as too "rough and tumble," note that research on purely playful "fighting" like this shows that it builds social awareness, cooperation, and altruism. You'll be doing everyone some good!

If lower-key, less messy, or more strategic fun is your style, organize something fun and unusual for the adults to do. How about a child-style party, where the adults go bobbing for apples, play Pin the Tail on the Donkey, whack a piñata, and play hide-and-seek outside? A yard-games tournament, to include croquet, boccie ball, badminton, and more? A scavenger hunt throughout your neighborhood? A board game festival to include Pictionary, Scattegories, Catch Phrase, and other laugh-out-loud games?

If you're concerned that the event might bomb, take note: the first time I organized one, I was worried, too. Yet because so many adults are trapped in mind- and spirit-numbing routines, many jumped at the opportunity to do something new, unusual, and fun. To see a group of adults finally let go and have fun just for the sake of it was a powerful experience indeed. Some very strong bonds and friendships were formed or reinforced there.

One final note: also consider inviting people you don't really care for or those who don't really care for you, such as certain family members, work mates, or neighbors. This is a beautiful way to experience different sides of other people and to form positive bonds where there were none. At the very least, you will get an opportunity to whack these people in the head with a tomato.

Intense Experience #2

୨

Dive Deeper into
Your Blood

To get the full value of a joy you must have somebody to divide it with.

—Mark Twain

Love takes off masks that we fear we cannot live without and know we cannot live within.

—James Baldwin

The first duty of love is to listen.

—Paul Tillich

If you want to go fast, go alone. If you want to go far, go together.

—African proverb

Many people who have gone through the 9 Intense Experiences say that this experience was *the* most, or one of the most, transformative of all. Many also say, however, that it was initially the most tempting to skip.

That's because if you just skim through the concepts that

underlie it, they may seem so obvious that it is easy to get fooled into believing this means you must already be doing it.

Yet what seems obvious when we finally take notice of it is usually the very thing we are forgetting and not taking enough action on. Forgetting what we already know is precisely how we screw our lives up.

For example, it is obvious that fewer high-calorie, high-fat, high-sugar, and highly processed foods and more fresh vegetables and lean sources of protein will help you live longer and better. But chronic disease from a poor diet is rampant, and 66 percent of adults in the United States are overweight.

It is obvious that getting plenty of sleep will keep you healthier and more energetic. But 50 to 70 million people in the United States alone are not getting enough sleep.

Immediate desires such as for French fries and soda pop and short-sighted choices like working more and sleeping less start as exceptions but become routine exceptions, which, of course, makes them the rule. What is obvious *when you are reminded of it*—eat right, sleep well—is very difficult to remain aware of and keep apparent in the choices you make. Our egos love to make our lives far more difficult than they need to be.

And so it is with family and close friends, your "blood." The theme of valuing and nurturing your relationships is used and abused to oblivion in greeting cards, TV commercials, politicians' speeches, and in other media far and wide. When you encounter it yet again, like a building you pass by every day, it is difficult to even notice and process it. And if you do notice it, it is easy to brush it off.

It probably seems obvious that building deep, meaningful bonds with your family and friends and striving to repair broken bonds that may be eating away at you deep inside are among the healthiest and most important experiences you can have in life.

Yet at epidemic levels in the United States and throughout the Western world, people feel lonely and disconnected. This applies to people of all ages, single people and married people as well.

People with families small and large. People who may interact with dozens or hundreds of other people on a daily basis.

This is not loneliness and isolation in the Robinson Crusoe sense of being physically cut off from others. It is loneliness of a more devious and arguably more destructive sort: feeling distant from and unknown, or not known enough, by even those who are most important to you. And feeling untrusting, or not trusting enough, of them, too.

Although you may not find it the most comfortable thing to do, carefully consider these questions:

- Do you often feel as if almost no one or no one at all knows the real you?
- How well do you really know the people who are most important to you? Do you know the one or two things they most dislike about themselves? The things they fear the most? Desire the most? Their biggest regrets? Their deepest beliefs on love and marriage, God, and where we go when we die?
- Do you often feel as if your relationships with others are not as close as they should be?
- How well do you really know what the people who are most important to you think about you? How would each of them describe your greatest strengths and weaknesses? Could they list your greatest fears, your biggest goals, and what you most dislike about yourself? Your beliefs on love, marriage, God, and where we go when we die?
- Do you often feel as if there are too few people, or there is no one, whom you can talk to openly about your interests, your passions, and your problems?

In 2006, the *American Sociological Review* released a report that Dick Meyer of CBS News said may be "the social health equivalent of the 1964 Surgeon General's report that declared smoking causes cancer." The report showed that feelings of social isolation had grown dramatically between 1984 and 2004. In that time period, for example, the number of people saying that they had no confidants—no one to whom they felt close enough to discuss important personal matters—had nearly tripled, to almost 25 percent of all Americans. Meanwhile, the number who said they had only one confidant had leaped to 19 percent. So 43 percent of Americans felt as if they had no one or only one person to whom they could really talk. Meanwhile, those who had four people they felt they could talk to dropped from 15 percent to 9 percent during the time period, and those who had five decreased from 18 percent to just 6.5 percent.

"But solitude can be very healthy," someone usually protests whenever I discuss this. Yes, solitude is a wonderful and necessary thing. But seeking solitude and its benefits is not the same at all as being lonely and isolated.

Seeking solitude is an active choice that comes from a healthy place; to step away from bonds with others to find peace and answers within yourself implies that there are strong bonds with others to step away from in the first place. In solitude, you may internally gather the deep and loving insights offered by others who are close to you, then sift through them to discover your own truths.

Meanwhile, no one actively chooses to feel lonely or isolated. Eliminating the feeling—and establishing deeper relationships that greatly improve all aspects of your life—can certainly be achieved if you actively engage in Intense Experiences, and if you also become aware of the insights into yourself that those experiences prompt. But the choices that lead to loneliness are passive; although they are indeed choices you made, you made these choices with other intentions, such as getting even more work done versus engaging with your spouse, children, parents, or siblings. Your intentions may have been good (working more to get a promotion, for example) but the consequences—increased distance from those who are important to you and heightened loneliness—are not.

"Well, it actually seems like we're all connected more than ever, not less," someone else will often state at this point when I discuss this topic.

Yes, with e-mail, texting, cell phones, and social media such as Facebook and Twitter, we have more *points of contact* than ever before. Yet as the breadth of our human contact has increased, the depth of our human contact has greatly decreased. We have far more blips of conversation with others—surface-dwelling chatter like "How are you?" and "I'm just so busy" and "I love Twinkies," as well as purely functional business talk. Yet we have far fewer deep and revealing conversations with anyone.

It is as if we each have a wheelbarrow full of fertilizer to nurture and grow our garden: our most important relationships. But many people are instead spreading their fertilizer across an entire hundred-acre field, where it loses the ability to nourish anything. Others, meanwhile, have thrown themselves into overworking, shopping, watching TV, and other illusions of comfort and are ignoring their wheelbarrow altogether.

How to Ruin Your Sleep, Worry More, and Feel Old

As research in neuroscience, health, and psychology is now demonstrating, this loneliness epidemic is one of the key causes—perhaps *the* main cause—of the record levels of anxiety and depression Westerners are facing. These feelings of isolation and loneliness are at the core of and also exacerbate the extreme stress, worry, fatigue, emptiness, apathy, and/or low self-esteem so many people suffer from.

According to Dr. John Cacioppo, a distinguished professor of psychology and director of the Center for Cognitive Neuroscience at the University of Chicago who is widely considered today's leading loneliness expert, this loneliness is killing people. It is doing so literally, because the consequential depression, anxiety, and other negative outcomes lead to chronic diseases such as cancer, heart disease, stroke, and all the rest that are so rampant. Because loneliness severely diminishes the quality of life, as well as the length of it, it is also killing people's productivity and creativity, their ability to succeed at life goals, and their happiness.

In Dr. Cacioppo's outstanding recent book *Loneliness: Human Nature and the Need for Social Connection,* he demonstrates that this deep disconnection from the people around us carries every bit the risk for chronic diseases and early death that smoking, obesity, and lack of exercise do. Among some of the most important findings from his research is that feeling detached and lonely can

- Significantly escalate premature aging, and increasingly affect people's health and well-being in negative ways the older they get.

- Significantly elevate levels of cortisol and epinephrine in the blood. The body produces these "fight or flight" hormones in reaction to stressful events and arousal, and although at normal levels they are beneficial, elevated levels can have very detrimental effects on your health. High levels of epinephrine can lead to restlessness, anxiety, serious sleep issues, and more. Elevated cortisol can lead to weight gain, high blood pressure, an impaired immune system, suppressed thyroid function, weak bones, blood sugar imbalances such as hyperglycemia, and more.

- Make people feel considerably more helpless, threatened, and stressed out in the face of challenges than people who do not feel lonely. Those who feel closely bonded to others handle the same level and type of stressful events much better.

- Turn molehills into mountains. That is, loneliness can prompt people to turn even small unfortunate circumstances into major catastrophes. (This, of course, further increases their anxiety, speeds up premature aging, weakens their immune systems, and further lessens their happiness.)

- Prompt people to make more reckless health and lifestyle choices than do those who don't feel lonely.
- Prompt people to feel less peace and joy from the positive events in their lives.
- Greatly reduce the energy replenishment and clarity provided by sleep, even when people are getting the same amount of sleep as those who do not feel lonely.

Other recent research has shown the devastating effects of feeling lonely and disconnected from people around you. A 2007 study by researchers at Rush Alzheimer's Disease Center demonstrated that lonely individuals may be twice as likely to get Alzheimer's disease late in life. And a 2005 study at Carnegie Mellon University in Pittsburgh found that lonely first-year college students showed a weaker immune-system response to flu shots than did other students. (To what extent can loneliness even impair the effectiveness of vaccinations and medications in other people?)

I have had the privilege of befriending Dr. Cacioppo, and one of the most crucial insights he has shared with me is that loneliness begets loneliness. That is, the family and the friends of people who feel disconnected and lonely tend to become lonely and disconnected as well. The societies they are a part of—the workplace, the school, the neighborhood, and so on—tend to push these lonely people to the margins and ignore them.

In other words, if you feel as if no one knows the real you, that you're misunderstood, or that you have few or no people you can really talk to about substantial things, chances are great that the individuals who are important to you feel the same way. This makes delving into the exercises in this Intense Experience and throughout this entire book even more important.

Another fundamental insight that Dr. Cacioppo has shared—and this may seem obvious, but is it also apparent in your life?—is that the quality of the time spent with your family is considerably more important than the quantity.

"This means not treating your time with family and friends as something to check off your to-do list," Dr. Cacioppo said, "but truly letting yourself go to being with them."

Sitting near your significant other as you tap away at a laptop computer while he or she stares at the TV is not enough. It is essential to give each other complete attention, to aim your noses right at each other and have deep, meaningful conversations.

Having unrushed and undisturbed contemplation sessions with themselves is challenging enough for most people today. Doing so with family and friends can be downright intimidating, even if it sounds obvious and right. That's because we live in a world that puts multitasking on a pedestal, as if it were some noble and worthy trait. (Studies show that multitasking is actually counterproductive, and that those who believe they are excellent at multitasking are actually the worst at it and produce lackluster results.) We live in a world that values getting everything quickly on demand, that praises just skimming the surface and going faster and faster, and that celebrates the processed and the humdrum in food, music, movies, TV, and more.

With all of these values so heavily weighted against having a deep connection with, and a deep awareness of, the others around you, it is little wonder that people are experiencing feelings of isolation, distance, and detachment with their family members.

Indeed, in terms of geography, technology, and more, human history has largely been a progression away from circumstances that enable and value deep, meaningful connections. This has occurred even as the population on the planet has exploded. As hunter/gatherers, people lived and moved in small tight-knit units. In agricultural societies, they still worked and lived very close together, in villages and small towns. But with the advent of cities—and trains and then automobiles—people drifted farther apart and spent more time away from their core units. The airplane extended this tendency to move apart. The rise of radio and especially TV increasingly turned even people who were physically dwelling in their core units away from one another and toward the boxes and the screens. Meanwhile, more women joined men in working outside of the home. Cities expanded to suburbs, which spread to the far suburbs known as exurbs, which added to the amount of time people spend in their cars traveling. Computers turned people's faces even more frequently away from one another and toward some screen, and then the Internet launched that into hyperdrive.

All of these inventions and shifts have their merits, of course. But encouraging people to slow down, to revere and savor, and to dive deeply into one another is not one of them. Even if you feel that you somehow share a lot of profound, meaningful words with loved ones via e-mail, texting, or on the phone, it is easy to forget that words coming out of your mouth or the movements of your hands are only part of human connection. More important are your body's gestures, facial expressions, and eye contact; the fluctuations and expressions in your vocal tone; your touch, ranging from handshakes to hugs to caresses; the physical energy that radiates from one person to another; and even the smells and the chemicals that work beneath conscious awareness.

Deep connection is a rare and endangered species, and more than any other factor out there, its absence is depleting people's self-esteem, motivation, productivity, health and longevity, and happiness.

The following exercises will quickly enable you to discover, or rediscover, the "obvious" benefits of nurturing deep connections with the important people in your life (and with your roots in general). You can

- Eliminate feelings of being lonely, isolated, unappreciated, and misunderstood.

- Improve your trust in those around you, and feel more trusted by them.

- Enable a greater sense of belonging and purpose.

- Build a stronger foundation beneath you to feel supported and more secure in all that you do and intend to do.

- Boost your self-esteem and your drive.

- Clear through self-sabotaging thoughts and emotions that so often stem from unresolved family conflicts, many of which you weren't even previously aware of.

The benefits you'll experience depend on who you are and what you are seeking. Yet one universal benefit is that you will have a deeper understanding of your own habits, choices, and personality. Such awareness is essential for many reasons, which include changing those things inside you that are holding you back from becoming who you know you really are.

Whether you have mostly dwelled on the surface with people who are important to you, or you already have some very close and meaningful relationships, the beauty is that you can always go deeper with other people. There are always powerful and life-changing benefits to be gained by doing so.

As you dive into these exercises, remember to carefully watch your thoughts and emotional responses. It is ideal to record what you experience after each exercise and ponder it all. The point is to benefit from these exercises immediately. Yet the *essential* goal is to discover which exercises—or variations of them—within these experiences work best for you, so that you can make their benefits a permanent part of your life.

Five Intense Questions for You

1. Whom do you wish you knew even better and felt closer to out of everyone who is important to you?

2. Make a list of all of the people you love. Why do you love each of them? What are some of the ways you show them?

3. Do you have secrets that you've never shared with anyone? Acts that you've done, desires or goals that you have, that you've kept to yourself, whether you consider them positive or negative? Why?

4. In terms of your beliefs, habits, and choices—such as in religion, relationships, politics, and career—how much of an influence would you say your parents' beliefs, choices, and habits were? How similar or opposite from theirs are yours?

5. Going 75 years back, 150 years back, and farther, do you know what the social status and the living standards were on both sides of your family? Were they mostly farmers? Merchants? Royalty? Did they live in cities, in villages, or on farms? And how might that history be affecting the way you think and what you believe today?

The Dive Deeper into Your Blood Exercises

Exercise 1: Take Someone Different to Bed with You Each Night

No, I don't mean like *that*.

For the next week or two, give gratitude to a different relative or friend each night before bed.

Spend at least a few minutes in solitude focusing your attention on someone who is or has been important in your life. Discover as many things as possible for which you are grateful to him or her. The big things and the little things, too—which, added up over time, are often the most important thing of all. The next night, choose a new relative or close friend to focus on.

For this particular exercise, it is especially important to write down what you are thankful for with each person. First, this physical act of writing will form a more permanent awareness inside you of what you are grateful for. Plus, it is healthy to periodically return to what you wrote about the person, especially when this individual gets on your nerves. Second, I encourage you to send each person you focus on a letter expressing what you are thankful for. Yes, you can convey it to the person live or via phone, but a written letter is a testament that carries a more powerful and permanent weight. It is something the person can and likely will keep for the rest of his or her life. Because we so seldom hear enough about how much we matter to others and why, receiving this letter can not only improve the person's day and week, but many times I have seen it improve the entire course of his or her life.

It is so easy to take people who matter in our lives for granted. In the frantic pursuit of fool's gold—going faster, working more— people forget the real gold that already surrounds them. When you don't nurture what you value, when you don't work to keep the obvious apparent, it can slowly slip away—or sometimes not so slowly. Then suddenly one day you awaken, and you wonder how you became so distant from what matters, including and especially the people who matter.

This exercise comes first in this experience because it is a rather rapid and powerful way to reconnect, or connect more deeply, to the people who really matter in your life—to poignantly remind yourself why they were so important in the first place.

When I have become stuck in certain ruts in my life, I have noticed that the predominant thoughts and emotions I feel for people I care about tend toward the negative, more than the positive. The more important the person is to me, the more negative the thoughts and the emotions are: what the person isn't doing to help his or her own cause or to help me; how the person isn't maintaining the household or the relationship. When we don't stay focused on the things we value the most, we tend to see what people we love are doing wrong, what they lack, versus all that they do right and everything we are thankful for about them.

Each night, pick a different family member or friend, and discover what you are thankful for about them. If necessary, tie a blue ribbon around your bedpost or put a picture of a family member on your washroom mirror to remind yourself to do this. By the way, I strongly suggest doing this exercise before bed, because dwelling on these positive, life-affirming thoughts and emotions as you settle in for the night will enable them to sink more deeply and permanently into your mind, heart, and being. The gratitude will be planted inside you, so to speak, and you will also sleep better.

Finally, it is important to mix it up. That is, when you are considering the various individuals who will receive your gratitude each night, choose the "obvious" ones—those you live with, such as your spouse, kids, parents, and so on. But also choose people who live far away, those you rarely communicate with, and even (and especially) who you hold grudges against or who may hold them against you.

Exercise 2: Explore These Films and More

During the next week or two, watch as many of the following films as possible. Read one or more of the books on the list. If there are other films or books centered on family relationships that you've been meaning to delve into, by all means do it during the time you spend on this experience.

Movies

Children of Heaven. An enchanting film that won prizes throughout the world, this Iranian film about the bond between a young brother and a sister may well prompt surprising insights about your own family relationships.

The Color Purple. If you've seen this masterpiece starring Whoopi Goldberg, Oprah Winfrey, and Danny Glover and directed by Steven Spielberg before, watch it again during the time you spend focused on this experience. The book by Alice Walker is also a masterpiece.

Crimes of the Heart. A must-see for everyone but especially sisters who grew up with sisters.

Dear Frankie. Single parents or those raised by single parents may particularly identify with this touching and intelligent gem.

The Dollmaker. An inspiring movie about the power of family, starring Jane Fonda as an imperfect but determined mother. Especially relevant to those whose families have or are enduring a great loss, such as the death of a child or an economic or natural disaster.

The Family Man. Nicholas Cage is at his best in this tender, funny, and wise tale about a fast-living, money-driven bachelor who is shown what his life would have been like—and can be like—if he chose diving deeply into family instead.

I Am Sam. A mentally challenged father, played perfectly by Sean Penn, seeks to regain custody of his daughter from the state in this film that epitomizes what deep love is.

I Never Sang for My Father. An award-winning film starring Gene Hackman, an especially good movie to see for anyone who grew up in a difficult relationship with his or her father.

Kramer vs. Kramer. This movie, starring Meryl Streep and Dustin Hoffman, won the Academy Award for Best Picture in 1979, and it is still widely considered the most honest and balanced portrayal of divorce and its impact on both spouses and children.

Marvin's Room. This is a must-see for anyone whose family feels fractured, with the members too distant from one another.

National Lampoon's Vacation. Watching this hilarious 1983 classic starring Chevy Chase and John Candy, you may find a surprising number of similarities between your family and the Griswolds as they cross the United States to visit Wally World.

Ordinary People. Those who come from or are in a family where the repression of thoughts and emotions is prevalent may especially relate to this film, which won the Academy Award for Best Picture in 1980.

A River Runs Through It. A gem directed by Robert Redford, set in the beauty of rural Montana, about two brothers, their father, and the true meaning of love and family connection. The autobiographical book by Norman MacLean is also exceptional.

Ulee's Gold. Peter Fonda won multiple awards for his acting in this must-see for people who believe they came from dysfunctional families, which means just about everybody.

Books

A Delicate Balance, **Edward Albee.** This is a Pulitzer Prize–winning play worth reading and seeing (and there's a good movie version starring Katharine Hepburn). From crumbling marriages to hurtful remarks that linger, everything about the challenges and bonds of family life is here.

The Glass Castle, **Jeannette Walls.** This beautiful memoir chronicles how the author found her way out of the oppressive influences of her strange and dysfunctional family and to her own truths, while still retaining love and gratitude for her family.

Loneliness: Human Nature and the Need for Social Connection, **John Cacioppo.** This is one of the most important books written in recent years. It eloquently presents a big-picture view of the loneliness epidemic, but it is also loaded with insights that you can apply to improving your own life, relationships, and happiness.

A Tree Grows in Brooklyn, **Betty Smith.** Although many novels have been written about family relationships, few have come close to the honesty and depth of this classic. The story is centered on the Nolans, a family trying to make it in the Brooklyn slums. You will likely experience many "aha!" moments in relation to yourself and your own family.

Exercise 3: Discover Those You Think You Already Know

Get to know at least three family members much better than you already do during the next week or two. Decide who, out of your immediate and extended family, you most want to know better. Give careful consideration to parents and grandparents, because their beliefs and choices can have such a powerful impact on your own. Also consider family members you are estranged from, passively or intentionally, because breaking the silence with them can open blocks inside you that you aren't even aware of.

The best way to dive deeper is through a live, one-on-one meeting or series of meetings, with each person, such as over dinner. Give the discussion ample time so that you are able to focus on each other, versus being distracted by other responsibilities. If geographical distance doesn't permit meeting in person, then a long conversation on the telephone with no time pressure or distractions is a good option.

Let each person know that your intention is to get to know him or her much better. If this is a family member you haven't spoken to for a long time, it may not be the easiest move to make—but now is the time. It is likely that deep down, this person yearns for a stronger connection as much as you do.

Have a solid notion of what you intend to discuss with each person before your conversations. You don't want the meeting to turn into an uncomfortable interview, of course, but have a good idea of what you'd like to talk about. Be prepared to have a *conversation*, though, meaning that topics will meander to unexpected places and you will be answering personal questions, too.

As with all of the exercises throughout this book, the main idea is that you will make the ones that most benefit you a permanent part of your life. Although so many people have veered away from depth with their loved ones, it likely is already obvious to you that this particular exercise *should* be routine in your life. Toward that end, I encourage you to check out the "Life Story Book," which is available on IntenseExperiences.com and which contains hundreds of questions worth asking of people who are important to you (and also worth answering yourself). For starters, though, here are twelve questions to consider asking people you choose for this exercise. These questions can open conversational doors wide and reveal new things about people who are important to you:

- What is the biggest goal you haven't yet achieved in life? Why haven't you?
- What are one or two of the hardest things you have ever had to do?
- What are one or two of your greatest accomplishments to date?
- Which one or two things do you most regret doing, or not doing, in your life?
- What are three things you fear the most?
- What is the most fun you ever had or one of the most fun things you've done?
- Which one or two periods or events in your life changed everything or a lot of things for you, turning you in a different direction for better or worse?
- Which character traits do you wish you had more of? Less of?

- Is there something you once believed in but don't anymore? Why?
- What are your beliefs about romantic love, true love, the idea of soul mates?
- How would you say people would typically describe you if you weren't around to hear them?
- And finally, ask whomever you are questioning how they would describe you to someone else who doesn't know you at all.

Exercise 4: Determine Your Character in Your Family Script

When people are young, they are almost always assigned a character role within their families. They may be assigned one role by their nuclear family, another often-similar role by their extended family, and yet another role that may be similar or completely different by their school friends.

If the roles are left unexamined, people can passively play these characters for the rest of their lives. They may subconsciously ignore desires and traits within themselves that don't jibe with their assigned roles and spend their lives feeling restless, incomplete, and incompatible with others without ever realizing why.

Just like characters in a play, these roles have their subtle complexities, which are unique to each individual, but for simplicity's sake, they can be summed up as a certain type.

For example, were you typecast as the smart one? The responsible one? The problem child? The loner? The funny one? The fragile one? The dumb jock? The geek?

Whatever the case, you were not then, just as you are not now, limited by any one or two of these roles. You have boundless potential, and your only limits are the walls you allow to be erected around you.

Tear down those walls!

You may come to realize that you like and choose some of the character roles associated with you. You will probably decide that you don't approve of certain other roles because they have limited you. The point is that you will be aware, and you will be actively determining who you are, versus passively playing roles that others assigned to you long ago.

Start by committing to be brutally honest with yourself. As an adult, especially one who has raised kids and even grandkids, you may find it mighty challenging to even agree to recognize that you might not have been entirely living your own life all of these years. Yet there is always more freedom to be gained and always more happiness to be had for that greater freedom.

Head to a private place where you can think clearly and not be rushed. Ideally, bring your journal along to write down your thinking process. And determine which roles you were assigned in the family and the social structures of your youth. While you are at it, figure out what roles you may have been assigned within your family and social structures today, including at work.

Most important, to what extent have you been living these roles? To what extent have they held you back? Have they held you back from having deeper relationships with family and friends, because you have played to these expectations of you versus being who you really are and therefore saying what you really need to say and getting what you really need?

This revealing exercise also offers another whopper of a benefit: it enables you to consider how you may be treating your family and friends according to their assigned roles and not based on the people they really are.

This exercise is a very powerful way to tear down walls inside you and walls within your relationships. Now, during this experience, is the ideal time to do it. Repeat it often throughout your life; when left unchecked, the walls have a sinister way of rebuilding themselves.

Exercise 5: Create Your Bucket List with Loved Ones

As popularized in the film starring Jack Nicholson and Morgan Freeman, a Bucket List contains the most important things you intend to experience and accomplish before you kick the bucket. Some items currently on my Bucket List include

- Learn to play the piano well, and create and record some original songs.
- Spend at least ten days frolicking in the Greek Islands with a woman I love.
- Write, coproduce, and codirect a musical based on this book.

Establishing such a list with your family is a fun and important exercise that can give each of you a deeper understanding of one another's goals and dreams. It is also a powerful way to remind yourself of what you value most. Furthermore, by sharing the Bucket List with your family, you can support one another's goals and dreams, which is part of what family is for.

When I was married and my son and stepdaughter were younger, we'd create and update our Bucket Lists on long car rides. We each took turns announcing an item on our list, with one of us writing down notes about each person's intention. Some items were things we intended to do as a family, and others were things we intended to do for ourselves. Because the kids were young, some of their intentions included getting high grades on tests or going on certain roller coasters they had previously feared. On subsequent long car rides, we'd revisit the list, adding new intentions and crossing off those we'd already accomplished or that were not so important anymore.

Just recently, I expanded this game by creating and sharing this Bucket List with my extended family, such as aunts, uncles, and cousins, via e-mail. We each wrote one item on our Bucket List and hit Reply All. It is a great way to get to know "distant" family members better and to make a workday more enjoyable.

Here are a few guidelines when creating your list:

- Add a date or a year that you would realistically like to achieve each intention by, to bring even more life to the list.
- Create two lists: those you'd like to do with your family and/or specific members thereof, such as your spouse, and those you intend to do alone (learning to play the piano, for example).
- Keep the lists that you and your family create accessible, so that you can revisit them often and support one another in achieving the goals described on them.
- Update your list routinely for the rest of your life. It gives you a concrete sense of purpose, which is one of the big keys to happiness.

Exercise 6: Indulge in Their Triumphs

An interesting thing happens when we witness other people's joy: it triggers the same areas in our brains as if we were experiencing the joy ourselves. That's why Hollywood, with its larger-than-life happy endings, rakes in the cash. We're not just spectators over here watching the happy ending unfold up there on the big screen. It is happening to us. At least, until the credits roll, the lights come on, and we have to detach. In Buddhism, this happiness at experiencing other people's happiness is called *mudita*.

On the flip side, studies have shown that what makes people in close relationships even happier than someone who is "there" during hard times is someone who is there to share their joys and triumphs. Experiencing a loved one's joy, in other words, is a beneficial and deeply bonding experience for both people.

With that in mind, this exercise is simple but powerful: during the course of this experience, go out of your way as much as possible to discover and point out your loved ones' successes and joys. It doesn't matter how small they may seem, we all experience some form of triumph every single day. Being aware of them is quite another story, of course; unless the success is monumental, people have a self-sabotaging tendency to focus on what went wrong, is wrong, or might go wrong. So make each of your loved ones aware, escalate their joy and yours, too, and enhance your bond with them, by recognizing and pointing out triumphs of theirs that they likely didn't even notice.

For example, ask about their day at work or school. But don't simply ask, "How was your day?" Ask instead, "What was the best thing that happened to you today?" This focuses their attention on the positive. Perhaps they finished a big project or are close to it, or maybe they got a good grade. Ask questions about these things, feel their sense of accomplishment, and congratulate them.

We tend to be most critical of ourselves. Next in line are the people we are closest to. Yet always pointing out the negative only begets more negativity and distance. For the one to two weeks of this experience, commit to making a vigilant effort to recognize and indulge in their positives. You'll experience some amazing changes by doing this.

Exercise 7: Call Your Dead Relatives

As strange as this exercise may seem to some people, it can be very powerful, revealing knowledge that is buried deep inside you, enabling you to release toxic thoughts and feelings, building and enhancing deep bonds, and more. Plus, it won't even cost you any cell phone minutes.

A physical phone is not required for you to connect with the dead, just as a ring is not required for you to be married. Yet seeing, touching, and using a physical symbol, especially one as relevant as an object that connects you with someone who is not actually right there, can help you tremendously in making that connection.

First, consider which departed relatives you intend to call. Think of those you were close to, or relatively so, with whom you may have unfinished business. What was left unsaid that should have been said? What questions do you have that were left unanswered? Do you feel as if these people held things inside that should have been spoken and asked, too?

Imagine that the dead can return for a conversation, and then have that conversation. Go someplace quiet where you won't worry about being interrupted. Sitting in a car in a parking lot works well, because no one can hear what you are saying, and you look like anyone else talking on the phone. Start the conversation just as you would with a living person you are close to whom you haven't spoken to in some time. It may feel odd at first, but stick with it.

If it helps, give the dead person the lowdown on your life: how your family is doing, where you are working, and the like. Perhaps share a favorite memory or two that you had with him or her, to loosen up the conversation more. Then say what you need to say. Ask what you need to ask. And listen. Your self-consciousness at how this is "weird" or "this isn't working" may try to get in the way sometimes, but be patient. Listen through those interruptions. From inside, you will hear the person's responses, and you will hear his or her questions for you, too. Respond, listen, question—you will gradually find the flow. And what you discover—what you come to find that you already know but were not entirely aware you knew—will likely surprise you.

Are you actually hearing what these relatives would say if they were alive? Or are you merely inventing what you want or need to hear? These are typical questions that can arise when you think about this exercise theoretically. When you *do* it, though, when you encounter the insights that occur when you speak with your dead relatives, you will see that these questions are not the point. Interesting questions, for sure, but they are irrelevant; the clarity, the release, the knowledge, the bond, and the other benefits are the point.

End the conversation when you are ready to end it. It can be quite emotional and therefore draining, especially initially. Yet the beauty is that unlike the living, the departed are always available when you need to call them again.

Exercise 8: Create a Perpetual Time Capsule

Someday you will be long gone, and everyone who knew you will be long gone, too. The farther forward time goes, the more you become merely a name and then not even that. (Now didn't that cheer you up?)

Yet although the memory of your body, mind, and name will fade, your spirit will linger on in the good that you have done and the knowledge you have shared. If you were allowed to come back five hundred years hence, you might be quite surprised to find remnants of your personal ideas, traits, quirks, and expressions lingering in your blood relatives.

You can "speak" even more directly to distant future generations of your blood—and help them, help your family now, and help yourself feel the timeless and centering power of connection across time and space—by creating a time capsule that can be updated within your family for eternity.

Imagine if you and your family were given this remarkable gift from your own previous generations. Visualize opening the time capsule and seeing and touching the mementos placed there by family members and the letters written to you from your relatives in centuries past. Now imagine your descendants one hundred, three hundred, five hundred years from now opening a time capsule that started with you and the mementos and the letter you included. Although you can only imagine receiving a time capsule from your previous family members, you can be the pioneer in your family who gives this amazing gift to future generations.

Here are the key steps:

- Get a large fireproof box that can be purchased at an office supply store or online. Consider decorating the outside of it with a family crest, surnames, and the like.

- Tape the key to the bottom underneath a memo noting that the box is not to be opened until you die, and that it is to be opened by your oldest surviving child or the oldest niece or nephew if you have no children (or designate someone else).

- Place a few key mementos of strong meaning to your family inside. These will be whatever feels most significant for your family's history, and your time and place in history, such as

  - Photos labeled with who is in the photo and the approximate year. Include pictures of your family as far back in time as possible, on through the youngest members of your extended family today.

  - A few key family heirlooms. Perhaps the outfit your grandmother wore as a baby when her parents immigrated from another country, the book your father wrote, or a watch that belonged to your great-great-grandfather. Whatever would connect your great-grandkids and their great-grandkids and beyond to their ancient family history.

  - A letter defining who your family members are, some key insights about each of their character traits and your own, and whatever else you want to share. Consider including major achievements and hardships that you and others in your family faced and describe how major historical events of our time, such as 9/11, that they may read about in their history books affected you.

- Also important is to leave a letter of instruction inside, telling whoever opens it that he or she is to leave your mementos and letter there and add some mementos and a dated letter of his or her own to it. This person should seal all of these items inside the box. On the person's death, an oldest child or niece or nephew should open it. Each generation should add to the box and repeat the process until the end of time. Somewhere along the way, of course, one of your distant blood relatives will have to get a bigger box. And one of them is going to have to remember to pack it when humanity moves to another planet.

Exercise 9: Be with Your Family

During the next week or two, as you delve into other exercises from this experience, intentionally escalate the amount of time you spend with your family in general.

If you live with family members at home, eat dinner around the table with them more often than you currently do. Invite family and friends who live in your area over for a barbecue. Play board games with them. Take walks with them. Hug, hold, and kiss them more, which has proved to reduce stress and increase feelings of well-being. It may seem obvious that this exercise alone can improve your mood and perspective tremendously and enhance your sense of connectedness and purpose, so make the obvious apparent. Although family members are all too easy to take for granted, they are one of our greatest gifts. Do enjoyable things with, and simply be with, your family more often.

Intense Experience #3

༄

Wander into the Forest, but Don't Bump into the Trees

Speak to the earth and the earth shall teach thee.

—Job 12:8

The wonder is that we can see these trees and not wonder more.

—Ralph Waldo Emerson

Each stone, each bend cries welcome to him. He identifies with the mountains and the streams, he sees something of his own soul in the plants and the animals and the birds of the field.

—Paulo Coelho

Consider your most recent experience when you spent some quality time in nature. Not thumping melons in the produce section or walking across your lawn to retrieve the mail, but quality time spent just *being* out in nature. Did you take a long walk in the forest? Follow a bug's dance through your garden? Let the waves hypnotize you from the shoreline?

Whatever the situation, recall how spending that time out in nature made you feel. Were you soothed? Centered? Revitalized? Unless a bee stung you, chances are good that the words you choose to describe how you felt are positive.

With that in mind, consider that according to the National Safety Council, people spend about 90 percent of their lives indoors. This startling statistic points to a clear and present danger on a number of fronts.

Maybe your typical experience with the outdoors is indeed only that place you pass through on the way to and from your car. But perhaps instead you are the rare person who gets outside more than just 10 percent of your time. Even if you are well outside of the norm, though, we're talking an *average* of 90 percent of time indoors. That number is not just extreme. It is utterly, ridiculously extreme. Unless you're the one dog musher who is officially employed by the U.S. government out of the 19.7 million jobs it provides, chances are great that you still don't get outside enough. Especially not outside in nature that hasn't been altered much by humans, such as forests, versus outdoor environments that have been modified, such as ballparks.

This 90 percent statistic points to a clear and present danger because, first of all, the air inside homes and other buildings is typically from two to five times more polluted than the air outside. Depending on the activity taking place, it can be up to a hundred times more polluted. All of that time you spend inside is clearly unhealthy.

Yet in terms of your mental and emotional health—and therefore your physical health, too, because they're all tied together—things get worse. Though you aren't typically conscious of it, when you are awake you constantly take in the experience of the shapes, the colors, the light, and the sounds around you. Remember: what goes into you—into your brain and heart through your mouth, skin, eyes, nose, and ears—is what you will get out of you.

Bland Colors and Dull Light

Look around yourself right now. If you are inside, chances are great that you are bombarded with rectangles and sharp edges. Look at the shapes of the walls, the floor, the floor tiles, the ceiling tiles, and the doors. The shapes of the windows, the couch, the bed, the tables, the desk, the shelves, the TV, the computer, the oven, the refrigerator, the books, and the outlet covers in the wall. You'll see an overwhelming number of rectangles, right angles, and sharp edges.

Now take a look outside. Not at the rectangular, sharp-edged buildings and other manmade structures, but at all of the things nature has created that haven't been altered (or altered much) by humans. You'll see trees, blades of grass, specks of dirt and sand, flowers, weeds, birds, bugs, squirrels, clouds, raindrops, hills, and streams—an abundance of curves, rounded edges, and soft circular shapes. The same goes for your own body.

To the human eye, the proportion of rectangles and sharp edges out in nature is far lower than all of the rectangles and the edges inside manmade structures. Although I haven't encountered any studies on this yet, it is only common sense: spending the great majority of your life indoors and having your senses continually exposed to so many rectangles and sharp edges cannot have a calming and centering effect on your heart and mind. On the contrary, it only contributes to your feeling, well, boxed in and edgy!

Now take a look around you, paying attention to the colors. If you are indoors, chances are great that only a few colors dominate whatever room you're in. They are likely "neutral" colors, such as off-white, beige, or gray. Even if there are multiple colors in your room and none of them are neutral, there are still only one or two shades of that color.

Now take a look outside. Not at the manmade structures, but at the vegetation, the dirt, the sand, the sky, and even the snow if 'tis the season. If all you see outside has pretty much been altered by humans, close your eyes instead and visualize the most unaltered places you've witnessed: the vast stretches of forest, prairie, mountains, and shorelines. First of all and depending on the season, there is likely a whole lot more blue and green out there than you are consuming indoors. Take a closer look outside, though: you will see myriad colors and infinite shades of those colors. Even the greatest painters cannot come close to capturing all of the shades of white in a cloudy sky or blue in a lake, which is why they try. The various colors and shades of those colors out in nature are infinitely more numerous than the colors in any room. Here again, common sense dictates that if you spend the great majority of your waking hours among primarily bland, neutral colors and relatively few other colors and shades of colors, compared to the great abundance in the natural world, you will feel much blander and less vibrant than you could and should. You are what you experience.

Now consider the artificial light inside your home, office, or any manmade structure versus the light from the sun outside. The unit light is measured in is called a "lux." When it's sunny, there may be more than 70,000 lux outdoors. When it is cloudy, there may still be 5,000 lux. Meanwhile, even "well-lit" offices and shopping malls have only 200 to 500 lux, and the light in a typical living room is a low 20 to 50 lux. By spending 90 percent of their time indoors, people are essentially living most of their lives in caves. In contrast, unless our ancient ancestors were sick or threatened by predators, they spent only their nights in caves, huts, and the like. Even worse, what little light you do typically get is artificial. Yet what your body, heart, and mind dearly need is natural light.

Experts overwhelmingly conclude that people are not getting nearly the amount of direct sunlight that they require. It has only made matters worse that people are intentionally hiding from the sun and slathering toxic sunblock on every moment they're exposed to sunlight, in a hyper-fear of skin cancer. Yes, too much direct exposure to the sun's UVB rays can be a risk. Yet it's the same as if people, concerned about air pollution, decided to stop breathing. Most experts now acknowledge that concern about sunlight and skin cancer has gone way overboard, exacerbating the already widely prevalent health issues that result from not getting enough natural light. In fact, Robyn Lucas, an epidemiologist at Australian National University, found in a recent study that far more people are dying from lack of sunlight than from too much of it.

Sunlight is the primary way your body gets vitamin D, which is essential for strong bones, a healthy immune system, a healthy brain, and a healthy heart. Vitamin D deficiency, which many experts say is at epidemic levels, can lead to Alzheimer's disease, osteoporosis, cancer, high blood pressure, heart disease, bacterial vaginosis, multiple sclerosis, seasonal affective disorder (SAD), and more.

Daniel F. Kripke, M.D., a professor of psychiatry at the University of California–San Diego and a pioneer in the research on light and health, has also demonstrated in more than twenty years of research that the extremely low levels of natural light people receive by being inside so much are linked to depression, anxiety, and feelings of lethargy.

Yet even without these studies, your body's intuitive knowledge and memory of how healthy it is to be out in the natural light prevails. Even if you limit your skin's exposure to direct sunlight to fifteen minutes per day and spend the rest of your time receiving natural light less directly under a canopy of trees, it will make you feel brighter.

Please Be Quiet

Noise pollution is one of the most serious issues of our time. You may be so accustomed to the damage it is doing to your mind, body, and spirit that you aren't even conscious of it, but in the manmade world, both indoors and in the outside parts of our world where human engineering dominates, there is now a never-ending cacophony. Growling cars. Screeching tires. Pounding construction. Roaring airplanes. Moaning pipes. Whining refrigerators. Blips, beeps, and dings from microwave ovens and computers. Plus, every annoying sound imaginable, and some unimaginable, from cell phones.

Try this little experiment right now: listen deeply. While for the sake of focus, sleep, or other forms of self-preservation, your brain tries hard to shut out those noises that aren't pertinent to you, take things in the opposite direction and try to identify every single noise you hear. The more you concentrate on doing this, the more sounds you tend to identify. In fact, depending on your location and the time of day, identifying all of the different sounds can seem impossible.

Constant sound of some sort from our environment has been prevalent one hundred, five hundred, and twenty-five thousand years ago, what with wind, insects, rodents, water, and everything else in constant motion. Yet the difference between then and now is the unending moan, cough, groan, and wail of manmade sounds that are ever-present almost everywhere today. Our brains and bodies were designed to be on the alert for raucous sounds—thousands of years ago, raucous sounds were exceptions to the comfortable "all is well" sounds of wind, waves, crickets, and chirping birds. Thousands of years ago, raucous sounds meant "Beware, hide from the growling lion," or, "Take cover, a thunderstorm is near," or "Run, a forest fire is approaching!" Today, there are always growling lions in the vicinity, constant thunderstorms nearby, and fires repeatedly approaching in the form of trucks, trains, airplanes, jackhammers, Vanilla Ice ring tones, and all of the other varieties of cacophony.

For this reason, too, it is no wonder that so many people feel stressed, depressed, and weary. It's no wonder people are so jumpy and angry. Some part of our brains must be working unnaturally hard at shielding our conscious awareness from this constant stream of raucousness—sounds that, in our natural state, would be few and far between and reserved for potential threats. Reading this now, you may think it makes sense in theory—yes, our brains may be overheating from repeatedly trying to barricade our awareness of noises that should be infrequent but are never-ending. Yet it is only when you finally spend time somewhere in nature, far removed from a manmade environment, where fewer cacophonic manmade sounds reach, that you realize—by contrast—how jarring, unnerving, and disturbing all of that noise back home is.

City Mouse, Country Mouse

As a child, I was fortunate to routinely experience these contrasts in sound—and in air, shapes, colors, and light—as I traveled between the manmade and the natural world and noticed the remarkably different effects they had on me. My grandparents lived on a farm next to the woods about sixty miles from the inner-city Chicago neighborhood I lived in, and I spent significant portions of my summers and other school vacations there with my sister. I became intimately aware of how nature calmed and centered me and how tension from arguments with my sister and other issues dissolved far more quickly out in the forests and the fields. The city is a box of concrete, metal, and noise that tends to hold all of its grudges and tension inside, but those same grudges and tension quickly blow away out in the open spaces. I recognized even then how nature made me feel far more boundless and free—so free that I often ran naked through the corn and the trees, allowing my body to experience the same naked joy as my heart and mind.

It is well documented that experiencing nature greatly reduces stress, improves energy levels, increases self-esteem, promotes creativity, and eliminates depression, while elevating feelings of joy and wonder. Great philosophers, spiritual teachers, and artists have extolled the unparalleled transformational power of nature ad infinitum. "Study nature, love nature, stay close to nature. It will never fail you," noted the architect Frank Lloyd Wright. "Man's heart away from nature becomes hard," said the nineteenth-century Native American chief Standing Bear. The great religions counsel the importance of getting out in nature, and many scientific studies verify that it is essential to physical, emotional, and mental health. A recent study even found that communing with nature not only makes you feel better, but also makes you *behave* better.

"Exposure to natural as opposed to manmade environments leads people to value community and close relationships and to be more generous with money," noted Richard Ryan, a professor of psychology, psychiatry, and education at the University of Rochester who led the study. Scientists are even finding that it may be literally uplifting for you to expose your flesh to soil, because soil contains microbes that stimulate the same neurons in your body that the drug Prozac does.

With all of that said, it seems almost ridiculous to have to make a case for *anyone* to experience nature more. Just as you may intuitively know that playing a lot in your life and spending quality time with your family and friends are remarkably good for you, you instinctively know that spending a lot of time out in nature is incredibly good for you. Our ancestors spent most of their lives outdoors, hunting, gathering, planting, playing, and relaxing beneath the sun and in the dirt. It's in our blood and being.

Yet here again, what you intuitively know versus what you routinely allow yourself to experience are two very different things. We spend 90 percent of our lives these days indoors. People's actions are way out of alignment with what their intuition knows is right, and that inevitably leads to depression, anxiety, restlessness, feeling overwhelmed, and all of the rest.

Wander into the following exercises to realign yourself. Wander into the soft shapes, the vibrant colors, the radiant light, and the sweet sounds. Wander into the forest. Mother Nature will quickly convince you of how transformative, centering, clearing, and inspiring she can be.

As you wander through her wonders and your big worries from the indoor world are brought down to proper size, just be careful that you don't get so giddy that you're tempted to forsake all human goals and duties and you end up bumping headfirst into the trees. Because Mother Nature is always ready to remind you of a beautiful paradox: that although you are of the water, the earth, the wind, the stars, and thus exist forever, you are also still of the flesh in the here and now. There is no such thing as a permanent escape to nature. The notion is romantic, but in hard ways, too, nature is always ready to remind you of who you really are. As documented in the popular book and movie *Into the Wild*, Christopher McCandless lost his life in the face of this lesson. Nature is instead there as an essential church to visit often to calm your spirit, to inspire your creativity, and to put what really matters—and what doesn't matter so much after all—back into proper perspective.

Five Intense Questions for You
1. When you were young, what was your impression of nature? Did you believe it was a wonderful place to be, was it foreign and mysterious to you, or did you dislike or fear it?
2. What have been your three most remarkable and memorable experiences out in nature? How did they make you feel during and after the experience, and how do they make you feel even as you sit here now recalling them?
3. Do you think it would be beneficial for your children, your grandchildren, or any other children you personally care about to get outside in nature more often? How do you believe it could benefit them? Do you think doing so would benefit you in similar ways?
4. Which type of natural environment are you most drawn to? A deep pine forest, the mountains, a desert, a jungle, or an island? Close your eyes and envision the place. Why

do you think you are most drawn to that particular natural environment?

5. What do you feel you might experience more of, and less of, by spending more time communing with nature?

Wander into the Forest Exercises

Exercise 1: Free Yourself from All Worldly Engagements

"I think that I cannot preserve my health and spirits unless I spend a day at least—and it is commonly more than that—sauntering through the woods and over the hills and fields absolutely free from all worldly engagements," wrote Henry David Thoreau in his essay "Walking." He continued, "When sometimes I am reminded that the mechanics and shop-keepers stay in their shops not only all the forenoon, but all the afternoon too, sitting with crossed legs, so many of them—as if the legs were made to sit upon, and not to stand or walk upon—I think that they deserve some credit for not having all committed suicide long ago."

Today, too, all of the service workers, the office workers, the home workers, and others who use their legs for little more than carrying them between rooms or to and from their cars—certainly not for taking walks outside—deserve credit for not having committed suicide or going nuts. Record levels of stress and depression and people complaining of feeling overwhelmed to the point of paralysis and zapped of energy and motivation do suggest, though, that the boundaries between sanity and insanity are getting quite thin.

Which brings us to one of the simplest but most important exercises from this and any Intense Experience: take as many long walks out in nature as possible. Specifically, try to take *at least* two hourlong walks "free from all worldly engagements" per week during the next two weeks. You'll find that it is far more beneficial than an hour you may typically spend watching TV or trying to get another errand done. "In every walk with nature one receives far more than one seeks," said the naturalist John Muir, and indeed, beyond the elimination of anxiety, depression, and anger and beyond the spark in your energy and creativity, you'll be surprised at what your nature walks will give you.

Yet there are a few important things to note. First, be sure that you are indeed free of all "worldly engagements" on your nature walks. Take these walks in solitude; as well-intentioned as other people may be, their perspectives and very presence on your walks can obfuscate what nature has in store for you. And leave your cell phone at home. If there is some particular issue eating away at you, leave even that issue at home; try to take your walk with only the intention of being out in nature to take a walk, not to think through or solve anything (you'll find that doing so actually clears away the clutter in your head and makes you far more effective at solving things later on).

As for where you take your walks, the more unaltered by humans the environment is, the better. But don't be discouraged if, for example, you live in the city, and walking through a neighborhood park is as natural as it gets. The main point is to escape from the confinement of walls and get out in the fresh air, beneath the open sky, and into the life beyond human life, even if it is life in its dormant winter state. Walking where there are even a few trees means walking amid healers.

If possible, vary the nature walks that you take. Yes, walking along the same path through nature has its advantages: for example, you always discover something new if you are open to it, and you experience firsthand that even familiar sights, such as a certain tree or the contours of the earth beneath your feet, are ever-changing through the hours, the weeks, and the seasons. But there is also much to be said for exploring the variety of natural environments to experience the impact of each of them. So, as much as possible, depending on where you live and your daily schedule, take a walk

- Surrounded by trees
- Along the sea or a lake
- Along a river or a creek
- In an open prairie

And pay attention to how these different natural environments affect your psyche and spirit in different ways. While you'll likely find that all of the environments can calm, center, and inspire you, you may discover that certain environments at various times provide you with specific benefits more than others. (It is certainly worth recording in your journal how a variety of natural environments affect you in different ways.)

Remember to be present on your walks. Keep all of your senses open to the natural world around you as you walk (doing so will stop your mind from creeping back to try to solve problems or worry about another item on your to-do list, among other benefits). Take notice of the small details, such as the patterns in the tree bark and in the swirling and lapping water and the remarkable variations in colors and shades, whatever the season. Listen intently to the sounds, such as the birds, the wind and the blowing snow, and the bug scampering up a tree. Inhale deeply; smell is a powerful primal sense and can work magic in its own right, so deeply breathe in the aromas of pine woods, rushing water, and a field of cattails. Touch and feel with intention. Follow your instincts to lie down in the cool grass or the warm sand, follow your desire to dip your toes in the water, and focus your awareness on the sensation of the cool breeze or the warm sun on your skin.

One more recommendation: weather and environment permitting, try to go barefoot on one or more of your walks, and, for that matter, go barefoot sometimes around your own backyard. Although we weren't born with shoes on, and for eons we as a human race experienced much of life with our bare feet touching the natural earth, today the average Westerner's feet almost never actually touch the ground. We spend most of our days in shoes, and when we're barefoot, it's almost always indoors, where we're walking on floors or lying on furniture. There are some who believe that the earth has a vital energy that we need to physically connect directly with, as is the case with all other land-based life forms on earth, and that the human disconnectedness with the earth is a key cause for our feeling overstressed, depressed, and otherwise imbalanced internally. Wearing shoes for most of our walking lives may also cause structural damage to the body, because we were born with feet that are best suited for our natural posture and gait. Several studies have indeed suggested that shoes may be detrimental to our health, including one published in the *New York Times*. There is actually an organization dedicated to going barefoot; for much more on this topic, visit the group's Web site at www.barefooters.org.

Exercise 2: Turn Nature On

Turn off the poison valves. Tune out the negative TV and radio programs that foster paranoia and disgust and would have you believe that hate rules and the sky is falling. To experience its unparalleled benefits for your mind, body, and spirit, turn nature on full volume. Increase the number of books and magazines you read, movies and programs you watch, recordings you listen to, and Web sites you visit that celebrate nature. For maximum impact, try exposing yourself *only* to these nature-focused media for a week or two, as much as possible.

Listen to CD and MP3 recordings of nature at home, at work, and in your car. One of my favorite series of CDs is called Echoes of Nature, and several of the best CDs in its line-up are *American Wilds*, *Ocean Waves*, and *Morning Songbirds*.

Watch nature-focused programs and read nature-oriented publications, such as the following top recommendations.

Movies

The Blue Planet: Seas of Life. From the producers of *Planet Earth* comes this breathtaking and inspiring journey into the marine habitats of our earth. Oh, the places you'll go with this ten-part series, which may well bring you to tears of joy.

A Day at the Beach. This is a movie of a different sort and one I recommend highly for this experience and whenever you want to relax and center. *A Day at the Beach* is one of the best in a series of movies that present the sights and sounds of nature in their original form, as if you were standing there experiencing them yourself. This movie provides ninety minutes of pristine beaches from dusk until dawn; meditate or pray with it playing in the background, read one of the following books with the movie on, or simply play it as you go about your business instead of having your TV tuned to bad news or the like.

Microcosmos. Via amazing camera technology and techniques, this masterpiece reduces you to the size of an insect and takes you deep into the insect world. If you think you're going to be grossed out, you may be in for a beautiful surprise.

Planet Earth: The Complete BBC Series. "Five years in production, over 2,000 days in the field, using 40 cameramen filming across 200 locations, shot entirely in high definition, this is the ultimate portrait of our planet," the packaging describes this eleven-part collection. And it is true. This is the most stunning and soul-stirring portrait of the natural world I've ever seen.

Winged Migration. This gorgeous film follows the journeys of various birds during their annual migrations. The film was shot on all seven continents during the course of four years, and the various vantage points that viewers are treated to of the birds in flight are simply stunning.

Books

The Earth Speaks, Steve van Matre. Dip into this exceptional collection of quotes, excerpts, and selections from some of our greatest nature enthusiasts whenever you want to refresh your soul.

Pilgrim at Tinker Creek, Annie Dillard. This Pulitzer Prize–winner is a series of interconnected essays that challenge the listener to contemplate the natural world beyond its commonplace surfaces. You'll learn how to feel and see even deeper.

Sand County Almanac, Aldo Leopold. Widely cited as one of the most influential nature books ever, it is as fresh and inspiring today as when it was published in 1949. Writing from the banks of the Wisconsin River, the author observes the natural world around him, elaborating deeply and eloquently on our place in it.

Walden, Henry David Thoreau. If you read only one book for this Wander into the Forest Intense Experience, make it this classic. Thoreau lived for two years and two months in relative isolation from the modern world in a small cabin in the woods near Walden Pond in Massachusetts, and this book, first published in 1854, tells that story. Far more than just an exceptional chronicling of the natural world he encountered, *Walden* is a deeply philosophical and spiritual book whose themes of personal discovery, freedom from prescribed rules and expectations, self-reliance, living simply versus being swallowed by an increasingly materialistic existence, and respecting instead of destroying nature are more relevant today than ever.

Also pick up a few copies of nature magazines or subscribe to them, such as *Audubon, National Wildlife, Nature Conservancy,* and *National Geographic.* Check out those dedicated to outdoor fun and living like *Outside*, and if you've ever pondered the joys of gardening, seek out gardening magazines; one of the best is *Green-Prints*, which through heartwarming stories about gardening and nature reminds you of the greater joy of simply being alive.

Finally, for inspiration, education, and amazing photography, delve into nature Web sites. NaturesBestPhotography.com has some of the most stunning nature photographs you'll ever see. And the Web sites of the various wildlife and environmental non-profits, such as OceanConservancy.org, NWF.org, SierraClub.org, Audubon.org, and Nature.org, are loaded with informative articles and gorgeous photos.

Exercise 3: Don't Eat What Your Ancestors Didn't Eat

The overall idea in this Wander into the Forest experience is to dramatically increase the amount of nature you take in, while reducing the amount of human-altered input, so that you will discover (or rediscover) nature's profoundly positive impact on your mind, body, and spirit. Although you consume nature through your eyes, ears, nose, and other senses, you also quite literally eat it. So for at least one week, eat no sugary cereals, corn chips, soda or diet drinks, or anything else processed, artificial, or otherwise altered by humans, and instead eat only all-natural foods that are as close to fresh and whole as possible. Though you may find it challenging at first, you will be quite surprised at how refreshed and energetic your body and mind will feel at the end of this exercise.

For a week or more, try to avoid processed foods, fast foods, microwavable foods, and foods and drinks that contain additives, preservatives, or extra chemicals of any sort. Eat only foods in their original state or as close to their original state as possible. Eat fresh vegetables, raw or cooked, as you prefer; fresh fruit, berries, and nuts; and cereal and breads made of all-natural products, including whole grains. Drink water and pure juice. If you eat meat, opt to eat chicken, beef, or other meat that has been naturally raised. The meat found in typical grocery stores today might as well be labeled "artificial," because the animals are injected with growth hormones to fatten them up quickly and antibiotics to keep them from getting too sick. The reason they're so prone to getting sick in the first place is that they're kept in cramped living conditions and they're force-fed diets that consist of foods they wouldn't naturally eat. Seek out meats labeled "all-naturally raised"; look for 100 percent grass-fed beef, for example, because cattle are grazing animals, and their natural diet is composed of grasses of various sorts. You can find these naturally raised meats in your local health food stores and on many Web sites, such as GrassfedTraditions.com.

If you already have a reasonably healthy diet, you may not find this exercise of going all-out-natural too challenging. If it does sound intimidating to you, though—if, for example, you're already getting the jitters at the thought of a day without your favorite soft drink—remember that there are more than 3,800 weeks in an average lifetime. You only have to try this for one of those weeks. There is a very good chance that at the end of this week, you'll more easily *want* to keep following a more natural and healthy diet, especially if you try these natural foods in concert with doing the other exercises in this experience. It certainly is worth trying.

Exercise 4: Make a Tree Your Best Friend

This exercise may seem normal to you, or it may be one of the weirdest things you've ever tried, depending on who you are, how you've lived your life and how you perceive the world, and how many illegal substances you've ingested over the years (just kidding, at least in some cases).

If you're in the "My God, this is odd" camp, good. Feel the fear, feel the weirdness, and do it anyway. Life is too short not to wander down the roads less taken, and in this case, I can guarantee that once you brush off those feelings of strangeness and embarrassment, you'll find it quite beneficial.

First, a few truths about trees. Trees are alive, and trees are giving. They're home to bugs, birds, rodents, and other life forms, and they give life to me, to you, and to most animals on the planet because of the carbon dioxide they consume and the oxygen they exude. Trees are also steadfast. They stand tall through thunderstorms, snowstorms, searing heat, and bitter cold, and even when their branches are cracked off or worse, they're committed to standing. And trees are not judgmental. You can tell them anything you've ever done or thought, and they will not criticize or shun you. They won't be swayed. They're like the best psychologists because you begin to feel so comfortable in their nurturing, steadfast, and nonjudgmental presence that you voice things you haven't been able to tell anyone else, and you hear yourself, often for the first time, recognizing and working through problems that have been festering inside you. As such, trees make exceptional friends. True, you can only imagine their stories, and they're not so much fun to watch a movie with, but you've got human friends for that.

So, go make a tree your best friend. Step out into your backyard or take a walk to a park or the woods and choose your giving tree. All trees are willing, and none of them will be hurt if you don't choose them, so just follow your intuition and choose the tree you're meant to choose. A stately oak? A fragrant pine? A sentimental willow?

Because you will be talking aloud to your tree, there may be some practical considerations to take into account when choosing your tree. You may be most comfortable with a tree that is out of public view, so that people walking and driving by, including the police, don't eye you with suspicion.

For anyone who already thinks this is weird, it's about to get weirder, but remember: people who recognize the fear or discomfort but don't cross the line anyway are those who stay stuck in ruts for life. So introduce yourself to the tree, and tell it how glad you are to have met it, because you are, aren't you? Then open your senses to your tree and get to know it. Trace the contours of its bark under your fingertips. Inhale the scent of the bark and the branches and, unless it has shed them for the winter, its leaves. Spread your arms, embrace the trunk of your tree, and feel the exchange of your life energies. Gaze up and know its main branches and smaller branches. Watch to see who some of its inhabitants may be, such as ants, squirrels, and robins. Then, standing or sitting, lean against your tree, close your eyes, and listen to its voice. How perhaps it creaks or its branches click against one another or its leaves rustle in the wind. Then embrace your tree again and let it feel your appreciation for it. If you are so inclined, as I suspect people who didn't feel weird about this in the first place may be, go ahead and kiss your tree (a friendly kiss, though, because this should remain a strictly platonic relationship).

Now that you've gotten to know more about your tree, find a comfortable position—standing before it, leaning against it—and reveal more about yourself to it. (For people who still feel uncomfortable that someone may be watching and judging you, even if you're burrowed deep in some woods, lean against your tree and flip open your cell phone, so that it looks like you're talking to someone on the phone and not to a tree. Your tree won't be offended.) Tell your tree whatever you are inclined to reveal: who your family and friends are, what you do for a living, your hobbies, how you're feeling that day, or whatever comes out that enables you to warm up to your tree.

Then reveal a secret. Go for the gusto and tell it something that you have long kept inside. Describe a past thought or action or words or actions done to you that have long squeezed you from the inside and stifled your spirit and potential. At this point, some people who have done this exercise in the past have noted a reluctance to voice their secrets because, even if they're in a secluded location with their tree, they feel watched. This is not so surprising because we live in an increasingly monitored society, so if that is the case with you, whisper your secret to the tree. Whisper it into your cupped hands, if need be. Just give voice to it before your new friend, this living, giving, steadfast being that will not judge you.

Let your words come pouring out. If anger flows, let it flow, and if tears flow, let them flow. Release all of the pent-up thoughts and emotions, and if those feelings of weirdness or paranoia resurface and interrupt, talk through them and past them. Open up, let it all out, and only when you feel that you've put it all out there for your tree, embrace it again. Thank it for being such a good listener, and conclude by pondering your tree. Notice how, no matter what you've revealed or confessed, it is still a tree. It is not leaning away from you in fear or pointing its branches at you in judgment or shaking its leaves at you in expectation. "Judge not, that ye be not judged," notes the Christian Bible, and although it is among the noblest of pursuits to strive to attain this state of nonjudgment, it is very difficult to achieve because we are all wrapped in our own fears and unexamined and unresolved issues. You can be sure that the more judgmental someone is, the more fear, anger, and other unresolved issues they have. Yet your tree's reaction to whatever you have revealed or confessed, the same as its reaction to anything that has ever happened to it or around it, is the most just response.

There at the base of your tree or back at home, you can choose to sort through all that you finally voiced. If there are any actions you realize you need to take to stand tall yourself and be who you are and move forward into living your life, such as seeking forgiveness or granting it or seeking professional help from a nonarboreal psychologist or the like, you can do so.

You can return to your tree again and again: to reveal other secrets that you have contained and that have held you back, to vent frustrations, to tell your tree jokes that nobody else seems to laugh at—your tree won't laugh either, but it won't judge you for telling such bad jokes—or simply to hang out to clear your head and spirit with a truly loyal best friend.

Exercise 5: Shoot Birds, Bees, and Flowers, Please

Ready, aim, shoot! With a camera, of course.

One of the most enjoyable ways you can wander back into nature, if you haven't been there in a while, or wander in even deeper, if you already go there routinely, is to grab your camera and/or video camera and go on wild shooting sprees. Even people who believe they don't have a creative bone in their bodies will discover that one hidden bone when they're equipped with a camera out in nature. You may not become the next Ansel Adams, but because every frame of the natural world is already a visual masterpiece, you may be surprised at the wonders you create with your camera.

Head to the woods, the desert, the shoreline, the park, or any natural area. Simply wander and let your muse guide you when you choose what to photograph and videotape. Try landscape shots like a snowy mountain range or the undulating water of a pond. Zoom in with close-up shots, such as the veins of leaves or the expression on a squirrel's face. Experiment with different angles and lighting on your subjects. The more your senses are focused on capturing these images, the more you'll notice in nature. You'll see shapes, colors, and textures you never paid attention to before. You'll find yourself favoring certain subjects and creating imagery that is a unique expression of who you are. You'll discover that you have your own style, and you can ponder that style—why you favor the subjects, the angles, the lighting, and all of the rest that you do—to find out more about yourself.

It can also be interesting to bring others along who will take their own photos and videos of the same natural area. Later on, you can compare what they chose to photograph or video record with what you did. Are there trends in terms of their subject matter, angles, and all the rest versus your own? And what might this suggest about each person's state of mind, personality, and values?

Alone or with others, when you spend your time photographing and video recording Mother Nature, it is a powerful way to experience her awesome ability to calm and center your mind, revive your spirit, spark your creativity, and learn, or be reminded of, who you really are. Plus, because you'll have photos and videos as a result, you'll be able to repeatedly revisit the serenity and the inspiration. I encourage you to post your best photos and videos on sites like Flickr.com and Photobucket.com and to e-mail me your most spectacular nature photos via the Contact Us area of IntenseExperiences.com, because I love sharing these with my newsletter readers. Who knows, you may discover that you actually are the next Ansel Adams!

Exercise 6: Plant Things and Grow Yourself

Ah, the beautiful and miraculous things we take for granted in this world, a world that so many people perceive as cold, dull, and difficult. Take a couple of deep breaths right now, open your mind, and consider the following as if you were learning it for the first time.

If you find a sunny spot outside during the warm weather months, and in that spot you dig a little hole in the soil, place a seed in that hole, refill the hole with soil, and then water that spot every day or so (unless the rain does it all for you), in a week or two, a plant will sprout up through that soil.

That this happens is utterly amazing. This creation of new life is the miracle of all miracles. It is still, and likely always will be, unexplained why this thing called life exists at all, whether it is our own life or any plant's, animal's, or being's on this or any planet. Yet because this unexplainable miracle is all around people every day, most don't recognize the wonder. Their attention is trained on finding what is bad and lacking, without noticing the abundance of what is good and right. Consequently, even as a bed of flowers or a tree grows right outside their windows, they shrink into physical clones of themselves, defined by their fear, anger, stress, worry, and emptiness.

Not you. Not with the 9 Intense Experiences and not with all of these exercises that will enable you to discover the positive, life-changing power of the experiences firsthand, such as this simple but profound exercise: plant something. Plant a single seed or multiple seeds, nurture the seeds as appropriate, and remain aware of the beautiful miracle of life as the seeds grow into plants.

What will you choose to grow? Enjoy pondering and planning this, because that choice, too, like all choices, reveals a lot about who you are and what matters to you. As the gardening teacher and author Sydney Eddison noted, "Gardens are a form of autobiography." (It also matters whether you will be planting and growing indoors or outside and which climate you live in.) Perhaps you'll grow tomatoes or other vegetables that you can harvest and appreciate eating. Maybe you'll grow one or more of the plants in the following Bring Plenty of the Outside Inside exercise that are exceptional for detoxifying your home, such as gerbera daisies. Perhaps you'll grow some visually stunning flowers, like begonias or lilies, or some highly fragrant plants, such as Russian sage or jasmine.

You can search online for tips on how best to grow whatever you want to grow. One of the most satisfying things about gardening is that unlike the human-invented world, where despite how hard you try, the outcome of things can seem so uncertain, when you plant a seed and follow the basic rules for growing that seed, it will virtually always turn out as expected. As sure things go, it is a sure thing, and that is a beautiful thing.

So choose your seeds, plant them inside or outside or both, water and nourish them as required, and let the plants' own growth remind you that you are witnessing a miracle, that you live in a world of remarkably routine miracles, that you yourself are also a miracle, and that life and the world are overwhelmingly full of good. You are now a gardener, which means you've joined the ranks of some of the earth's happiest people.

Exercise 7: Be a Dirty Volunteer

Get your hands dirty. Get your knees dirty. Get a bunch of plant stuff in your hair—and love it.

One of the most rewarding exercises you can do to intimately experience nature and its benefits, while also helping to protect it now and for the future, is to volunteer for any of the nature-oriented organizations that need your help.

Most areas have public forests and nature preserves, and they are always seeking volunteers to help remove invasive plants, harvest and sow seeds, and more. Here in the Chicago area, for example, Friends of the Forest Preserves (www.fotfp.org) seeks volunteers to help preserve the sixty-eight thousand acres of forested land in and around the area, and they even certify some people to work the woodlands, the wetlands, the savannas, and the prairies.

Maintaining 193 million acres of forests and grasslands throughout the United States, the U.S. Forest Service (www.fs.fed.us) is always seeking volunteers, as is the National Park Service (www.nps.gov), which manages the United States' nearly four hundred national parks. National nonprofits like the Nature Conservancy (www.Nature.org) are always seeking volunteers for a variety of hands-on work. And most national forest and park services and organizations of other countries throughout the world similarly seek volunteers.

If you'd prefer to do work in or near oceans, lakes, rivers, and other bodies of water, there are many organizations seeking help, such as Clean Ocean Action (www.CleanOceanAction.org), the Ocean Conservancy (www.OceanConservancy.org), and Thank You Ocean (www.ThankYouOcean.org).

Finally, if getting your hands really dirty by farming interests you, many organizations are looking for volunteer help on farms throughout the world. Check out www.GrowFood.org and the World Wide Opportunities on Organic Farms' Web site at www.wwoof.org.

Whatever type of natural environment you want to work in, or whatever specific type of wildlife you may want to work with, such as bears or wolves, do a Google search for it, and you will discover organizations that need volunteers. You'll find that the time and energy you spend out there in nature gives a spirit-lifting gift right back to you.

Exercise 8: Bring Plenty of the Outside Inside

Although you'll want to get out in nature much more frequently, it is also very healthy for your mind, body, and spirit to invite much more of nature inside your home and office.

Start with what you consume endlessly: air. The heavily insulated walls, roofs, doors, and windows that are prevalent today may make homes and offices more energy efficient, but the superinsulation also imprisons the dust and the chemicals from carpets, furniture, copiers and printers, household cleaners, plastics, and so on, inside manmade structures, causing today's dangerously high levels of indoor air pollution. As often as possible, open your windows and doors to let in the fresher outside air and the sunshine, too.

Fill your home and office with detoxifying houseplants—about one per every hundred feet of space is ideal. In 1989, NASA published the results of a two-year study demonstrating that houseplants can be an effective weapon against indoor air pollution. NASA conducted the research, along with the Associated Landscape Contractors of America, with the goal of learning how to create healthier interior living spaces on earth and in space. The study particularly focused on houseplants' effectiveness in reducing three major indoor pollutants: formaldehyde, which is contained in carpeting, cleaners, foam insulation, fire retardants, and more; benzene, which is emitted from inks and dyes, plastics, detergents, and more; and trichloroethylene, which comes from dry cleaning, inks and dyes, adhesives, paints, and more. Seven of the houseplants that were most effective at detoxifying these indoor pollutants can be found on this page.

In addition to cleansing the air, houseplants add soft shapes and rich colors to your home and office, thereby alleviating the stress caused by so many squares and sharp edges and the tedium that results from so many bland neutral colors. Houseplants add growing life energy to interior spaces that can otherwise seem dead, and it is life that you can see, smell, and experience by watering and caring for your plants.

There are many other ways to bring nature inside your home and office to inspire creativity, relaxation, and positive energy. An abundance of fresh-cut flowers, dried flowers and plants, and fresh fruits and vegetables should be as essential in your life as coffee and toilet paper. Toss out artificial soaps and household cleaners laced with toxic chemicals, and opt for those with all-natural ingredients instead. Indulge your home with natural scents such as lavender

---

Seven of the Healthiest Household Plants

Bamboo Palm

Chinese Evergreen

Gerbera Daisy

Janet Craig

Marginata

Peace Lily

Pot Mums

and mint from potpourris, essential oils, and candles (be cautious of typical candles because they contain unhealthy paraffin wax; opt for nontoxic candles made from beeswax or organic soy wax). Fill the empty spaces in your home with paintings and photographs of landscapes and other natural scenes, including your own pictures from the earlier exercise in this experience.

Another powerful way to channel the calming, centering, and inspiring power of nature directly into your heart, mind, and spirit is to listen to sounds from nature at home, at the office, and in your car. Because it is more likely that you'll hear engines or horns than waterfalls and crickets outside your windows, definitely invest in CDs and MP3s that provide a long duration of soothing sounds from nature, such as Echoes of Nature recommended earlier. Even better to start or end your day are DVDs that present scenes and sounds from nature together, such as *A Day at the Beach*, also recommended earlier. Of course, you can play your own audio and video recordings that you created of your favorite natural places in exercise 5 of this Wander into the Forest Intense Experience.

When you bring more nature inside, as with all of the other exercises, be sure to be self-aware; pay attention to how this alters your moods, your energy levels, and your perspective on the issues, goals, and values in your life. By *doing* the exercises, and by being aware of their inevitable and incredible benefits to you—versus merely being told about them—you'll truly "get" why you'll want to make this Intense Experience a permanent part of your happy and successful life.

Intense Experience #4

၆

Ignite Yourself with Genius

We must overcome the notion that we must be regular. It robs you of the chance to be extraordinary and leads you to the mediocre.

—*Uta Hagen*

The reluctance to put away childish things may be a requirement of genius.

—*Rebecca Pepper Sinkler*

Thousands of geniuses live and die undiscovered—either by themselves or by others.

—*Mark Twain*

Neither a lofty degree of intelligence, nor imagination, nor both together go to the making of genius. Love, love, love: that is the soul of genius.

—*Wolfgang Amadeus Mozart*

There are endless lines we are told we cannot cross, or should not cross. What is beyond those lines?
"I don't care," mutter the masses.
"Probably a threat!" shout the warmongers.
"I don't know, but I'd like to know," respond the thinkers.

"Perhaps something good," say the peacemakers.

"I don't know, but I intend to find out," exclaim the enlightened. And when they persevere in doing so, they are the geniuses.

You have some form of genius in you. I know you do because I have yet to meet anyone who doesn't have some remarkable gift waiting to burst forth. Most people never realize their gifts, though, because it is hard to find the inspiration to courageously cross the lines they've been warned to stay inside from godlike entities in their youth, such as parents, clergy, teachers, and other guardians of social convention, and from unassailable authorities in adulthood, such as the media, their bosses, the government, and so on. It is even more difficult to find the inspiration to persist in remaining outside those lines to pursue their gifts when there are no safety nets, they receive little or no encouragement, and usually criticism or downright hostility is being launched at their backs.

You probably already have a good idea of what your remarkable gift or gifts are (there are likely more than one). Your remarkable gifts may be something you can make a career out of, or enhance your career with, or they may promote your inner peace or improve your relationships. Genius need not be something that is financially profitable or public. Your remarkable gifts are whatever you have dreamed of doing or becoming in those times where your mind and spirit have transcended lines of complacency and fear—fear of failure, of being criticized, of losing a steady paycheck, or of not fitting in with the averages.

Where does that inspiration come from—the courage to step outside the lines that others have drawn for you, for their own benefit or based on their own fears? Where can you tap into that even greater inspiration to persist at realizing your dreams and gifts, despite the fear and the criticism?

Having delved this far into the book, you already have the answer. The inspiration to become who you know you are meant to be comes from within, and it is fed by Intense Experiences that charge your being and keep your heart, mind, and spirit wide open to the wonder and gift of being alive.

If you try to maintain that inspiration to live your life deeply, honestly according to who you really are, and therefore happily, but you limit yourself to repeating mediocre experiences, is like trying to keep a bonfire blazing by feeding it only toothpicks. Impossible.

What you feed your flame determines how brilliantly it will blaze. What you put in you is what you will get out.

Mediocrity in, Mediocrity Out

You win a weeklong, all-expenses-paid trip, and you are given the choice of one of three lodging options. The first option is a five-star resort with breathtaking views, 1500-thread-count sheets on the beds, award-winning restaurants, and all of the other luxuries that will revive your spirits. The second option is a standard hotel, clean enough, with a queen-size bed, cable TV, and continental breakfast in the morning that includes apple Danishes. The third option is a run-down motel with a bed whose springs are about to explode out of the mattress and whose walls are so thin, you can hear the thoughts of the man in the next room, and those thoughts aren't good.

Which of these options do you choose?

Most people, given the equivalent choice of a five-star resort versus the standard or substandard in other areas of life, are overwhelmingly choosing the standard and even substandard, although the price they'll pay for the five-star choice is often far less! That's largely because they aren't aware that five-star options that will ignite their being are even available to them, they don't realize how aggressively and surreptitiously the mediocre choices are being pushed on them for other people's gain, and they are clueless about how negatively those mediocre choices are affecting their lives.

Why settle for top ten songs that the big record business executives have decided to repeatedly ram into our ears, when so much brilliant and beautiful music of genius from all genres is just an iTunes search away? Why turn on the paranoia-inducing, mind-numbing, formulaic mush the big television executives are pushing on prime-time TV, when so many mind-expanding and inspiring films and programs await in video stores, online, and right there on other channels of your TV? Why eat processed, chemical-laced glop in pretty packaging that the big food industry executives have decided to shove down your throat on grocery shelves, in fast-food restaurants, and in never-ending ads everywhere, when so many mind-, body-, and spirit-nourishing foods of genius are (affordably) available at fruit markets and in responsible grocery stores and restaurants that deserve your business?

Shopping itself is marketed as the international pastime, the thing to do when you've got time to do something. The masses fall for this marketing and fall because of it, even though a world of Intense Experiences awaits them—experiences that will stir their souls and help them achieve the success and happiness they were meant to have.

Yes, some of what is mass-produced and mass-marketed is very good and even exceptional—my Apple MacBook Pro is a work of beautiful genius, for example. Yet far more of what is mass-produced is mediocre at best, and your dreams and spirit are worth far more than that.

What you put into your being, what you spend your time and energy doing, and what you consume with your mouth, eyes, ears, heart, and brain determines how you feel and what you will produce, create, and achieve. If it is mediocrity in, you'll naturally feel mediocre and project mediocrity outward.

Mediocrity is not synonymous with less expensive, just as the fact that something costs more doesn't mean it's better. In a recent study, participants were first told how much several bottles of wine cost, and then they were asked to taste the wine. Not surprisingly, they overwhelmingly said they preferred the considerably more expensive bottle. Yet two weeks later, without knowing which wine they were trying this time or how much it cost, they were again asked to taste the wine and state their preference. This time they overwhelmingly preferred the cheapest wine! All that glitters is certainly not gold.

Another important side note: it can be worthwhile to the spirit to occasionally consume junk. I certainly enjoy mind-candy movies and TV shows and real candy like Hershey's bars sometimes. But you already know what happens if you eat junk food frequently, especially if you aren't eating the healthy stuff far more often to offset it. Your body, mind, and therefore spirit increasingly suffer for it. You sabotage yourself. It is no different than if you routinely, versus sparingly, feed your brain, heart, and spirit a diet of junk. You sabotage your growth, happiness, and success—your ability to become who you already know you are meant to be.

Mozart Fuel or Muzak Fuel?

Explore the background of any person who has achieved success in a particular area, from sports to business to the arts, and you will discover that one key to that success has been immersing himself or herself in the works of genius of people who have come before in that area. Stephen King immersed himself in the works of Edgar Allan Poe, H. P. Lovecraft, and J. R. R. Tolkien, among other geniuses of horror and fantasy writing. Beethoven immersed himself in the works of Mozart. Expand this concept, and it only makes sense that people who achieve overall success in their lives are very aware of, and particular about, what they choose to allow into their heads, hearts, and spirits and what they bypass. Oprah Winfrey famously immerses herself in books that have either already proved to be works of genius or that her staffers suggest may be brilliant. Throughout adulthood, Abraham Lincoln read voraciously the works of bona-fide geniuses such as Shakespeare to nurture himself.

As with anything that's true, once you become aware of it, it just seems like common sense: by choosing to immerse yourself in the greatest works and feats of others—in film, music, literature, cuisine, fashion, and other arts, and in areas such as science and sports, too—versus mediocrity, the more fuel you'll have to ignite the greatest aspects of yourself.

A question I often hear when I present this experience in live training is "Who really decides what are works of genius and what are not?"

I will be the first to agree that there are many beautiful works of genius that never saw the light of day or that didn't remain in that light, due to political, financial, or other influences. And, of course, what may resonate deeply with one person may not with another. The recommendations in the following exercises are those that time and consensus have largely confirmed are works of genius. Still, they are only recommendations. The list is anything but all-inclusive, and you are encouraged to delve into other works recommended by any individual or group you trust.

Okay, then, ready? Ignite!

Five Intense Questions for You
1. Do you believe you have some remarkable gift residing in you that has not been fully brought to light?
2. In what areas of life are you consuming mediocrity, which could be replaced with beautiful works of genius that would enable the best of you to emerge?
3. What one book, film, and piece of music would you call the greatest work of genius for how it inspired, challenged, and perhaps changed you? Branch out further: what one performance in sports that you've experienced would you call the greatest feat of athletic genius? What one architectural wonder, poem, painting, play, sculpture, speech, political act, live musical performance, scientific discovery, and/or business move would you say is the

greatest work of genius you've ever experienced within those fields?

4. Have you personally ever known someone you would call a genius? What makes that person so?

5. What remarkable gifts do you think the people you most care about each contain within them? Have you told them?

The Ignite Yourself with Genius Exercises

Exercise 1: Rekindle Everything You Ever Dreamed of Doing

Before diving into others' beautiful works of genius, grab your journal or something to record your list on, find a quiet place to be in solitude, and open your dream doors wide. Starting with the present and working backward to your youth, what are the things you have ever dreamed of doing, being, creating, and accomplishing? I don't mean merely your goals in your job or those nagging items lingering on that endless to-do list, such as updating your résumé. I mean things that filled you with inspiration, hope, and life, however "foolish" or "impossible" you (or other people) may have convinced yourself they were.

Here are a few of my own:

- Hosting an Intense Experiences festival, where people come for three days and are immersed in a range of musicians, authors, performers, personal growth and health speakers, interactive experiences, and more, and leave deeply inspired and equipped to become who they know they're really meant to be

- Hosting a TV show that similarly focuses on people, events, and other experiences that profoundly motivate and equip people to become who they know they're really meant to be

- Opening an Intense Experiences theme park with a layout similar to Epcot Center that achieves on an even grander scale what the festival will

First, let your list flow, without thinking much about each item. When your list is finished, go back and consider each item with the following questions in mind:

- Does this dream still excite me today?
- Is this dream still something I could *possibly* do? (In my case, I dreamed in my youth of becoming a major league baseball player, but I am clearly past the years where that's possible. My knees insist that is so. So that dream will continue to live itself out only inside me, where I always hit a grand slam with a 3-and-2 count in the bottom of the ninth, with the entire World Series on the line. Yes, in my mind I am that good.)
- Which of these dreams *most* excites me today? You can rank each item on your list on a scale of one to five, with five being the most exciting.
- Out of those that most excite me and that I could still possibly do, what is really stopping me from pursuing the top one or two? Not the excuses, such as money, time, kids, or responsibilities, but the real reasons behind those excuses. I must remember that excuses will always be plenty, but this is my one life, and I am setting an example for others by what I choose to do.

Perhaps you are already pursuing your dreams. If not, though, surely there are one or two on your list that you can strive for. Now is the time to begin. But instead of letting my words inspire you, only to have that inspiration fade, start taking those first steps with your dream as you dive into the rest of these exercises. The inspiration will come from within you, versus from outside, and I can assure you that the inspiration will therefore be much deeper and more permanent to drive you forward. To prevent the waning of that inspiration, persist in this and other Intense Experiences that most resonate with you long after you finish this book.

Exercise 2: Invite the Speech of Angels In

Music is well said to be the speech of angels; in fact, nothing among the utterances allowed to man is felt to be so divine. It brings us near to the infinite.

—*Thomas Carlyle*

Thomas Carlyle wrote this observation in the eighteenth century, and it is still among the most potent things ever written about music. Of course, anything written or said will never really do justice to music, because music transcends language and thought and goes straight to the spirit. No matter how much certain brilliant scientists try to disprove the existence of spirit, in fact, the far more brilliant music will be there to prove those scientists wrong.

For this exercise, immerse yourself in the brilliance, and go for the new and different. Even though I hope you already listen to music that you consider inspired by genius, for the next several weeks immerse yourself in brilliant music that you've never or rarely been exposed to. In your car, at home, in the office, let the speech of angels you haven't listened to before move you. Because most people today primarily listen to R&B, hip-hop, rock, pop, and country, especially consider delving into classical music and jazz, where arguably the greatest musical geniuses ever have shined. If you currently thumb your nose at rock or country, however, thumb-wrestle your thumb down with your other thumb and open your heart to masterworks in those areas. Just try it. All genres of music and all of the pieces considered masterpieces within those genres will not resonate with everyone. But you will be surprised at how some music you've never really listened to before resonates with, and expands, you. I can assure you that the more you immerse yourself in new musical works of genius, especially outside your customary domain, the more amazing self-discoveries you will have.

Classical Music
Mass in B Minor and Toccata and Fugue, Johann Sebastian Bach
Messiah, George Frideric Handel
The Planets, Gustav Holst
The Rite of Spring, Igor Stravinsky
Symphony No. 5, Gustav Mahler
Symphony No. 6 (*Pathetique*), Pyotr Ilich Tchaikovsky
Symphony No. 9, Ludwig van Beethoven. Many call it the great-
    est music ever created, and I agree. Also try Beethoven's
    Symphony No. 5 and Violin Concerto.
Symphony No. 41 (*Jupiter*), Wolfgang Amadeus Mozart, which
    many others call the greatest music ever created, and I also
    agree.

Jazz
25 Greatest Hot Fives & Sevens, Louis Armstrong
Brilliant Corners, Thelonious Monk
Getz/Gilberto, Stan Getz and Joao Gilberto
Kind of Blue, Miles Davis. Widely considered the greatest jazz
    album ever.
A Love Supreme, John Coltrane. Along with Miles Davis, Col-
    trane is considered the greatest among jazz greats. But his
    work, including this one, can be challenging to those who
    are newer to jazz.
Maiden Voyage, Herbie Hancock
Mingus Ah Um, Charles Mingus
Saxophone Colossus, Sonny Rollins
The Shape of Jazz to Come, Ornette Coleman

Sunday at the Village Vanguard, Bill Evans
Time Out, The Dave Brubeck Quartet

Opera
Opera can initially be challenging for those unaccustomed to it, but try at least two. I encourage you to go online or read a book for background on whatever operas you delve into, to get an overview of the stories they are telling. Here are several that are considered among the all-time greatest and are also quite accessible to people who are not yet opera aficionados.

Die Walküre, Richard Wagner
The Magic Flute and *Don Giovanni*, Mozart
Rigoletto, Giuseppe Verdi

R&B/Soul
Best of the Atlantic Years, Ray Charles
Lady Soul, Aretha Franklin
Songs in the Key of Life, Stevie Wonder
What's Going On, Marvin Gaye

Country
At Folsom Prison, Johnny Cash
No Fences, Garth Brooks
Red Headed Stranger, Willie Nelson
Roses in the Snow, Emmylou Harris

Blues
Pretty much anything by:
Buddy Guy
Howlin' Wolf
Leadbelly
Muddy Waters

Vocal
Pretty much anything by:
Nat King Cole
Ella Fitzgerald
Etta James
Frank Sinatra

Popular / Rock
Are You Experienced? Jimi Hendrix
Born to Run, Bruce Springsteen
Dark Side of the Moon and *The Wall*, Pink Floyd
Exile on Main Street, The Rolling Stones
Highway 61 Revisited, Bob Dylan
The Joshua Tree and *Achtung Baby*, U2
Led Zeppelin IV, Led Zeppelin
Legend, Bob Marley and the Wailers
London Calling, The Clash
Nevermind, Nirvana
OK Computer, Radiohead
Pet Sounds, The Beach Boys
Purple Rain, Prince
Rumours, Fleetwood Mac
Sgt. Pepper's Lonely Hearts Club Band, *The White Album*,
    Revolver, and *Abbey Road*, The Beatles
The Sun Sessions, Elvis Presley
Tapestry, Carole King
Thriller, Michael Jackson

Exercise 3: Read the Masterpieces, Unveil the Truth

"Fiction reveals truth that reality obscures," noted Ralph Waldo
Emerson. "Fiction is the truth inside the lie," Stephen King

reiterated a century later. If you don't currently read fiction, perhaps because you don't believe it is worthwhile or English classes
in school prompted you to equate reading fiction with hard work,
try to wash yourself of those notions and give it a chance for this
experience. Read at least one of the masterpiece novels—consider
those that are most accessible from the following Level 1 list—and
read several short story masterpieces. If you already read fiction
and you like a worthwhile challenge, consider reading one or two
books from those at Level 2 or even Level 3 and several short story
masterpieces during this experience. The greatest fiction can reveal
and illuminate the human condition, and particularly your human
condition—the complexities of the head, the heart, the body, and
the spirit—in a way that other modes of communication cannot.
That way is by telling a story, and stories are as old as humanity
itself. When a story is told well, you are no longer a reader outside
the page reading for knowledge; you are a being within the story
itself, experiencing it all and discovering wisdom to make your
path clearer firsthand.

Novels
Level 1—Short and Relatively Easy to Read
Dubliners, James Joyce
Of Mice and Men, John Steinbeck
The Old Man and the Sea, Ernest Hemingway
O Pioneers! Willa Cather
Sula, Toni Morrison

Level 2—Mid-Length and Somewhat Challenging
Adventures of Huckleberry Finn, Mark Twain
Captain Correlli's Mandolin, Louis des Bernieres
The Grapes of Wrath, John Steinbeck
The Road, Cormac McCarthy
Their Eyes Were Watching God, Zora Neale Hurston

Level 3—Long and/or Most Challenging

Any William Shakespeare play, particularly *King Lear* or *Hamlet*

Crime and Punishment, Fyodor Dostoyevsky

Gulliver's Travels, Jonathan Swift

Moby-Dick, Herman Melville

The Sound and the Fury, William Faulkner

Short Stories

"Barn Burning," William Faulkner

"Gift of the Magi," O'Henry

"Good Country People," Flannery O'Connor

"The Jilting of Granny Weatherall," Katherine Anne Porter

"The Lady with the Dog," Anton Chekhov

"The Lottery," Shirley Jackson

"An Occurrence at Owl Creek Bridge," Ambrose Bierce

"The Things They Carried," Tim O'Brien

"Where Are You Going, Where Have You Been?" Joyce Carol Oates

"A Worn Path," Eudora Welty

Meanwhile, "Poetry is nearer to vital truth than history," said Plato. I almost placed reading poetry under the previous musical exercise, because the greatest poetry is music played with words, amplified by your brain, and heard in your heart. People are often concerned about "getting" poems in a rational sense, but like music, a great poem works because it is felt in the heart and the spirit. Don't worry about overanalyzing it and having it make sense in your head. Pick up a collection of the greatest poems from the bookstore or the library, and just read one here and there that calls out to you—reading it aloud versus in your head is by far the best way to experience the poem.

You can also find the following beautiful poems online, and I strongly recommend that you read these, even and perhaps especially if the idea of reading poetry doesn't thrill you:

"The Act," William Carlos Williams

"The Bells," Edgar Allan Poe (definitely read this one aloud!)

"A Contribution to Statistics," Wislawa Szymborska

"Dust of Snow," Robert Frost

"Incident," Countee Cullen

"I Saw in Louisiana a Live-Oak Growing," Walt Whitman

"Love after Love," Derek Walcott

"An Ox Looks at Man," Carlos Drummond De Andrade

"Ozymandias," Percy Bysshe Shelley

"Time," Louise Gluck

Exercise 4: What's Your Rosebud?

Although I have urged you to turn off your television throughout this book, I must note that the medium of TV has produced many works of brilliance. There is true genius, for example, behind *Seinfeld*, *All in the Family*, *The Twilight Zone*, *60 Minutes*, *Hill Street Blues*, *Star Trek*, *Alfred Hitchcock Presents*, and *The Oprah Winfrey Show*, to name a few shows.

Yet in the United States, the average home has more TVs than people, and the average American watches 153 hours of TV per month, which is 1,836 hours of TV per year! So much for the common complaint that there is never enough time to do the important things that need to get done. And while I will recommend it in the Laugh It Off Experience in the next chapter, I hardly need to suggest watching TV to anyone. Instead, at least for the two weeks or so that you immerse yourself in this experience, forgo TV shows altogether. Instead, try to watch only the greatest films of all time. If you did no other exercise but this one, I can guarantee that you would experience some very perceptible and positive shifts.

In combination with the other exercises here, though, the shifts will be astounding.

Do a Google search of the phrase "greatest films of all time," and you will find many lists containing different film masterpieces. Such lists, like mine, are, of course, subjective. You'll also find certain films consistently repeated in list after list, such as *Citizen Kane*, *8½*, *Casablanca*, *Schindler's List*, *Bicycle Thieves*, *The Godfather*, and *Lawrence of Arabia*. These films are like Shakespeare's and Dostoyevsky's greatest works in literature: so consistently cited that their greatness is indisputable. Don't miss them. (If you watch *Citizen Kane*, you'll also get the title of this exercise.) That said, you really can't go wrong with any of the following films. Not all of them will resonate with everyone, but whatever genre these films get filed under, they transcend it, and they can transform you.

8½ (1963)

The 400 Blows (1959)

2001: A Space Odyssey (1968)

The African Queen (1951)

Amadeus (1984)

Apocalypse Now (1979)

Bicycle Thieves (1948)

Bridge on the River Kwai (1957)

Casablanca (1942)

Cinema Paradiso (1988)

Citizen Kane (1941)

Closely Watched Trains (1966)

Crouching Tiger, Hidden Dragon (2000)

Days of Heaven (1978)

Fanny and Alexander (1982)

Full Metal Jacket (1987)

Gandhi (1982)

The Godfather Part I and *Part II* (1972, 1974)

Gone with the Wind (1939)

GoodFellas (1990)

Grand Illusion (1939)

The Grapes of Wrath (1940)

Groundhog Day (1993)

Hoop Dreams (1994)

Il Postino: The Postman (1994)

It's a Wonderful Life (1946)

The Killing Fields (1984)

Lawrence of Arabia (1962)

The Lord of the Rings Trilogy (2001, 2002, 2003)

Life Is Beautiful (1998)

Network (1976)

Night and Fog (1955)

Pan's Labyrinth (2006)

A Passage to India (1984)

Platoon (1986)

Raise the Red Lantern (1991)

Rocky (1976)

Schindler's List (1993)

Seven Samurai (1954)

Shawshank Redemption (1994)

Thelma and Louise (1991)

The Thin Blue Line (1988)

Saving Private Ryan (1998)

Shoah (1985)

Singin' in the Rain (1952)

Star Wars, The Empire Strikes Back (1977, 1980)

Unforgiven (1992)

Vertigo (1958)

West Side Story (1961)

The Wizard of Oz (1939)

Exercise 5: Culture Yourself

"As the soil, however rich it may be, cannot be productive without cultivation, so the mind without culture can never produce good fruit," said the Roman philosopher Seneca. Music, literature, and film are typically the most accessible means of cultivating your being, because they can be brought into your home, car, and place of work. During the course of this experience, though, try to get out as often as possible to experience other forms of culture, particularly those you rarely or never seek out. Remember, now is the time to open your heart and mind; if you thought you were never particularly interested in dance or art, now is the time to expose yourself to the best of it. You might be surprised at the transformative power of an art form you've always ignored.

If you live in or near a city, this exercise is easier to accomplish, but if you live far from one, consider making at least one or two trips and trying several new cultural experiences while you are there.

Research online for great plays being performed in your area, and read what the reviews say about them. Definitely seek out a Shakespearean play. Try to see a ballet or a modern dance performance. Take an architectural tour, and visit botanical gardens and Japanese gardens. Visit museums that showcase works of genius in science and technology. Go to an opera, a jazz performance, and a classical music concert.

And be sure to visit art museums. When you do, find a painting or a sculpture that calls you into it. As you gaze on it, first simply let yourself feel it. Become aware of thoughts and emotions that it is pulling out of you. Ask yourself why it is doing so, how it is doing so, and what it is about this particular piece of art that calls to you. What is the painting or the sculpture about? What are its dominant tones, colors, textures, and shapes? Why do its subject matter, theme, colors, tones, textures, and shapes resonate with you? In the same way that there are reasons well worth understanding why, say, a seashore calls out to your spirit more than an evergreen forest does, there are reasons well worth understanding why a certain masterpiece calls out to you more than others do. Go to an art museum, find your favorites, open yourself to why they are so, and you will find more of yourself.

Exercise 6: Chew Genius Slowly

The average meal lasts eleven minutes in the United States, with some breakfasts and lunches lasting only two minutes. Meanwhile, in many other countries, meals can last for hours. In our go-go-faster-faster culture, dominated by myths of convenience, food has been demoted to the status of functional fuel. In fact, if you taste-test any processed meal out of a cardboard box or a plastic bag against a meal consisting of fresh ingredients and prepared lovingly by a chef or a family member, you'll notice that it literally *tastes* like functional fuel.

For this mouth-watering and eye-opening exercise, try to eat and drink *only* works of genius for the next couple of weeks. Yes, that may require you to go on a fun and productive grocery-shopping trip and/or treat yourself to some very good restaurants!

When it comes to food, nature is the ultimate genius. Step away from the go-go-faster-faster life that blinds people to the miracles all around them, and consider nature's genius: from apples, garbanzos, and kumquats, to pecans, shiitake mushrooms, and zucchini, nature provides nearly infinite masterpieces of taste and nutrition for us to choose from. When you step back and really consider this, it is quite strange and even morbid that people choose Quarter Pounders and Sprite in such abundance over these delicacies.

Whether shopping for yourself or eating meals prepared at a restaurant, choose only foods made from fresh and natural ingredients. Try to avoid mediocrity—processed foods and drinks—for this exercise.

If you eat sweets or baked goods, avoid the stuff in cardboard and plastic, and head to a local bakery where they use only fresh ingredients and love to prepare the pies, the cakes, the cookies, and all of the rest.

If you drink beer, ditch the mass-processed stuff, despite their funny commercials. Head to your local store and treat yourself to several different master-crafted regional brews; many liquor stores sell them by the bottle, so you can try different kinds. If you drink wine, tea, or coffee, do the same thing; if there is a specialty wine shop or tea house near you, head over there, because you'll find experts who can give you great recommendations.

Visit your local produce store and stock up on your favorite fruits and vegetables, to eat in their natural state or add to any recipes you cook up. Here, too, expand your horizons; try fruits and vegetables with weird colors, shapes, and names that you've always passed by and wondered about. Adzuki beans. Lychee. Ugli fruit.

When it comes to cereals, breads, cheeses, and all other foods, choose only the whole, natural, old-world-crafted and lovingly prepared kinds. Avoid additives, preservatives, and colorful toucans.

If you eat out, treat yourself to only the good stuff. If you can afford it, try the gourmet restaurants in your area that get all of the great reviews. Sometimes, a restaurant's popularity turns out to be merely hype, but more often, the food is indeed exceptional because the chef behind it pours passion, perseverance, years of experience, and seemingly miraculous knowledge of his or her ingredients and how they mix—that is, genius—into his or her culinary creations. That said, a restaurant meal doesn't have to cost your next paycheck to offer you the exceptional. There are many mom and pop restaurants, ethnic restaurants, and even a few places that offer you food fast—although it is anything but fast food—and are extremely affordable. In the north suburbs of Chicago, for example, the Pita Inn restaurant in Wheeling, Illinois, which specializes in Middle Eastern cuisine, offers some of the best-tasting entirely fresh food I have ever eaten anywhere; the typical entrée is less than eight dollars and is served in about five minutes. These sorts of places exist everywhere. Research your area restaurants online or, even better, ask neighbors and friends for their recommendations, and you will find them.

Most important, whether you eat simply at home, take the time to prepare elaborate recipes, or eat out, slow way down. For the duration of this experience, give yourself more time to eat. Take time to savor the food's appearance and smell and to chew it deliberately, which allows you to experience much more of its taste. (Chewing your food slowly and longer also releases more nutrients to benefit your body and can contribute to weight loss!)

Finally, if you are reading this and experiencing resistance—you may think that you don't have the time to eat deliberately, or that consuming only exceptional food and drink is "splurging"—remember again that what you put in is what you will get out. As you will discover, this exercise will boost your energy levels, improve your mood and focus, and therefore increase your productivity, self-awareness, and happiness.

Exercise 7: Let the Mystery of Your Night Dreams Guide You

Science has yet to conclude what dreams are or why we have them. Sigmund Freud theorized that dreams represent our unconscious thoughts and desires. Another theory is that dreams provide a sort of therapy, allowing the dreamer to work out issues in a safe environment. A different hypothesis holds that dreams are a way to clear the brain of clutter, like cleaning your computer's memory so that it functions better.

Yet one thing is certain, according to recent research: the majority of people believe dreams are useful and provide insights that can help them in life. Therefore, what is far more relevant than what dreams may actually be is what people believe they are, because when people believe in something, whether it is love, religion, or four-leaf clovers, that belief gives something real back to them. And because dreams can be so rich, varied, and strange in story and emotion, they are a vast breeding ground for self-reflection, interpretation, and answers.

You can likely recall dreams you've had that provided you with insights about issues you were facing and perhaps even specific answers or gifts. In a dream, golfer Jack Nicklaus discovered a better way to hold his golf club that improved his game. The tune for the Beatles' song "Yesterday" came to Paul McCartney in a dream. Elias Howe perfected the invention of the sewing machine due to a dream. And Madame C. J. Walker, cited in the *Guinness Book of World Records* as the first American female self-made millionaire, founded a very successful African American cosmetics company. By 1917, she had the largest business owned by any African American in the United States. The ingredients for the hair tonic that made her famous and successful came to her in a dream.

That dreams can be such rich fodder for insights, solutions, and gifts is reason enough to pay close attention to them. And as you may have already experienced in your life, when you go to sleep after immersing yourself in something positively or negatively intense that day, or when you sleep during longer periods of intensity, your dreams are often at their most vibrant.

So, while immersing yourself in genius-inspired music, literature, films, culture, and foods during the course of this experience, try to recall your dreams first thing every morning. One way to remember to do this is to place a journal on top of your alarm clock every night, so that when you reach for the alarm, touching the journal will immediately signal you to recall your dreams. It is, of course, strongly recommended that you write down your dreams as soon as possible, because the very act of writing will help you recall more details of the dream. And then ponder those dreams.

You will find that concentrating intently on experiencing beautiful works of genius in your free waking hours can trigger not only your inspiration and brilliance during the day, but some mighty amazing night dreams, too. Brilliance begets brilliance. Whatever challenges, goals, and dreams you are pursuing during the day, such as the dream you may have decided to focus on in the first exercise in this chapter, after reflecting on your night dreams it is almost assured that you will discover profoundly useful gifts. The more you realize those gifts within your dreams, the more excited you will become about dreaming—and about waking up in the morning and recording and reviewing those dreams. As with the other exercises in this book, by delving into this one intentionally now, you'll naturally want to do it for the rest of your life.

Exercise 8: Become a Phonophile or an Oologist

I'm not suggesting that you pursue questionable activities here. I'm urging you to start a new collection of things that might really interest you.

A phonophile collects phonograph records. A bestiarist collects medieval books on animals. A plangonologist collects dolls. And an oologist collects bird eggs. If none of those objects excite you, there are nearly infinite things out there that you can collect. What really fascinates you? What in relation to that can you see yourself collecting?

Human brilliance has been poured into the creation of every type of object imaginable. Teddy bears, watches, bookplates, shoes, music boxes, and even key rings—the collectors of those are known as copoclephiles—all have their masterpieces, and to truly open your mind and gaze on any one of these is to experience the whole of human passion and perseverance concentrated into this one metaphor.

Whether you choose to collect things made by human ingenuity or by the genius of nature—collectors of shells, every one of which is a masterpiece, are known as conchologists—collecting provides you with something else to be passionate about in this world. Collecting is a form of gratitude, as you acknowledge that the world and everything in it is a wonder and a gift, including this object that you have decided to focus on. Collecting also relaxes you and reduces anxiety. Seeking that special something to add to your collection creates a greater sense of purpose. It opens doors much wider to social interaction with, and recognition by, those who collect what you do. And because there is a world of stories and knowledge contained in anything—stamps, old photographs, rocks, toys—collecting exercises your imagination and keeps your brain young. Finally, on the purely practical side, certain collections can become financially valuable. For example, marbles are hot now, and one little marble called the Onion Skin Blizzard Marble recently sold for nearly $10,000! Or you can become an online expert in your collectible area or open a museum.

Tom Hanks collects vintage typewriters. Billy Dee Williams collects cookie jars. Bob Barker collects military figures. Those are rather common collectibles, but what other people collect can be quite amazing. A man named Graham Barker collects navel lint, and now, according to the *Guinness Book of World Records*, has the world's largest collection (implying there are others!). A man named Martin Mihal has collected about forty thousand chocolate wrappers from around the world. You can visit his online museum at www.chocolatewrappers.info, if this somehow interests you.

A collection doesn't have to consist of physical objects. I collect quotes, as you may be able to tell from this book. Some photographers specialize in collecting specific expressions or events, such as people kissing or sunsets.

So, what's it going to be? Porcelain figures? Nature sounds? Vintage tennis rackets? Doughnut holes? Now, while you're engaged in this experience, is a perfect time to start your new collection.

Exercise 9: Glimpse Your Own Genius Again

I opened this chapter by noting that everyone has some form of genius inside him or her. But I've certainly heard the arguments against this notion: if everyone has the potential of genius, it cheapens genius itself, and besides, with the overwhelming predominance of mediocrity and stupidity in the world, everyone is clearly not a genius.

Yet just because something lies buried doesn't mean it is not there. We are all born with remarkable gifts of some sort, but years and decades of rust and crust from living according to others' expectations bury those gifts. The commitment to becoming who we really are and venturing into the experiences that will reveal our true selves and help us achieve our goals and dreams will enable us to clear through that rust and crust. I am not suggesting that everyone can be an Einstein or a Mozart, because there are neurological bases such as bigger brains for certain kinds of towering intellectual and creative genius. But I am stating that given the immense range of gifts a human being can possibly have, and given the infinite types of human endeavor that these gifts can be applied to, everyone does have some form of genius residing in him or her.

If you believe this completely or you doubt it—but especially if you doubt it—I encourage you to again go to a quiet place with pen and paper where you can be alone and focus. Now walk backward through your life to answer this question: where have you already shined the brightest?

No matter what your age or circumstances, you have already received at least some glimpses of your remarkable gifts. Because no matter how deeply they may be buried, these gifts are illuminated, they shine as bright as the sun, and, given the right experiences, their light breaks through the rust and the crust. You may simply be suffering from Muddy Slope Syndrome so much that you fail to recognize and remember. Another reason you might not recognize your gifts is that you may be defining what is worthy of being called a gift through society's eyes, instead of through your own. American society currently elevates pop singers and musicians, movie and TV actors and actresses, athletes in certain sports, business magnates, certain politicians, and, to a lesser degree, doctors, lawyers, authors, painters, photographers, and architects, for example. Because there is great money and loud applause at the highest levels of these particular endeavors today, far too many people believe that those are the *only* areas in which human talent and genius shine, and they hitch their dreams and self-esteem to them, only to have those dreams and their self-esteem crushed. Meanwhile, no one is similarly noticed and exalted for being a remarkably gifted parent, caretaker to special education individuals, customer service agent, auto mechanic, or herb gardener. Yet despite the lack of public adoration, accomplishment in these areas is no less remarkable or noble.

Carefully review your life. Whether it is within some area of work, your ability to nurture people emotionally, how you engage with certain animals, or any other human endeavor, where have your various remarkable gifts already shined through? How do these gifts correspond to the first exercise in this experience of pursuing your dreams, and how do these gifts relate to the goals and the path of your life right now? Are you staying true to these gifts to fortify your spirit and achieve deep inner peace and happiness, even if billions of dollars and cheers from the masses won't necessarily follow? Do you want to?

"If a man is called to be a streetsweeper," Martin Luther King Jr. said, "he should sweep streets even as Michelangelo painted, or Beethoven played music, or Shakespeare wrote poetry. He should sweep streets so well that all the hosts of heaven and earth will pause to say, 'Here lived a great streetsweeper who did his job well.'"

Intense Experience #5

✬

Laugh It Off

Laughter is an instant vacation.

—*Milton Berle*

At the height of laughter, the universe is flung into a kaleidoscope of new possibilities.

—*Jean Houston*

With the fearful strain that is on me night and day, if I did not laugh I should die.

—*Abraham Lincoln*

When people are laughing, they're generally not killing each other.

—*Alan Alda*

Knock knock.

Who's there?

Ima.

Ima who?

Ima author, I hope you like my book.

Okay, maybe that didn't floor you. But kindergartners love it! They're an easier audience, though: according to Dr. William Fry, an emeritus professor of psychiatry at Stanford University and an expert on the relationship between laughter and health, kindergarten students laugh an average of three hundred times per day. Adults, meanwhile, laugh only about seventeen times a day. Yet although there certainly is a lot to laugh about in the kindergarten years, life only gets far more absurd and amusing as we grow older—if we maintain a healthy perspective to see it that way. This is one of the most poignant statistics I've ever encountered, which confirms that adults are running themselves ragged, cramming themselves with mediocrity, experiencing spiritual constipation, and taking everything far too seriously.

Almost everyone has heard the saying "Laughter is the best medicine," and while some might argue that Viagra is even better, the saying holds immense truth. As usual, though, just because something makes perfect sense when you read it or rationalize it doesn't mean it is being put into action. Again, the average adult laughs only seventeen times per day, when at least three hundred opportunities are available—and probably many more.

Recall a time when you've recently laughed. Or better yet, here's a joke that might do the trick for you now:

A man who was called to testify at the Internal Revenue Service asked his accountant for advice on what to wear. "Wear your shabbiest clothing. Let him think you are a pauper," the accountant replied. But when he asked his lawyer the same question, he got the opposite advice. "Do not let them intimidate you. Wear your most elegant suit and tie." Confused, the man went to his priest, told him about the conflicting advice, and requested some resolution of the dilemma. "Let me tell you a story," said the priest. "A woman, about to be married, asked her mother what to wear on her wedding night. 'Wear a heavy, long, flannel nightgown that goes right up to your neck,' her mother replied. But when she asked her best friend, she got an opposing opinion. 'Wear your sexiest negligee, with a V-neck right down to your navel.'" The man protested to his priest, "But what does all this have to do with my problem with the IRS?!" "Simple," said the priest. "It doesn't matter what you wear, you are going to get screwed."

It feels good to smile and laugh, doesn't it? It's a powerful and delightful way to blow away all of those ashes of challenging and stressful situations that would otherwise build up into rust and crust inside you and make you anxious, weary, unproductive, sick, and generally not very nice to others and especially to yourself. In the case of the previous joke, Americans laugh because we all feel tension even at the mention of the IRS; if you're from another country, instead of the Internal Revenue Service just substitute whatever governing body overtaxes you and spends your hard-earned money foolishly, and you'll laugh, too.

During and after smiles and laughter, you can just *feel* that they are exceptional medicine. Your body and spirit know this. Scientific research in the last thirty years has pinpointed the astounding range of laughter's benefits. According to a University of Kentucky review paper of some recent scientific studies, laughter can

- Improve your blood pressure
- Decrease the hormones related to stress in your body
- Increase your infection-fighting antibodies and fortify your immune system
- Relax your muscles
- Reduce pain you may be experiencing
- Improve your brain function
- Restore your respiration, sending more oxygen-enriched blood and nutrients throughout your body
- Help prevent heart disease
- Provide a good cardiac, abdominal, head, and back workout
- Enhance your emotional health
- Rejuvenate your energy
- Improve your relationships

Interestingly, even just anticipating a good laugh—for example, by embarking on the following exercises—has been shown to have health benefits, such as boosting health-promoting hormones and decreasing stress-inducing hormones!

These are amazing benefits for something that feels so good and that is so widely and instantly available. Laughter is the epitome of both preventive and curative medicine. In fact, if you want to solve any challenge, internally or with someone else, you are highly advised to first find the humor in the situation and laugh about it. As the frowning mask and the smiling mask symbolize, tragedy and comedy come from the same mold. It is a spirit-clearing and emotionally relieving experience to see your own challenges through the eyes of the smiling mask. It's not always easy to slip on that mask, of course, but as another saying goes, laughter is contagious. When you are down, you are assaulting your body and soul if you don't expose yourself to a binge of whatever makes you laugh. And even if you aren't down, you are putting your body and soul at great risk if you don't routinely—far more than seventeen times per day—find reasons to laugh.

Drop DeGeneres Bombs

Laughing even if you don't find something funny, laughing just to laugh, has also been shown to be beneficial. There is a growing trend called Laughter Yoga that incorporates yogic breathing and laughing for no reason (although a reason quickly presents itself, which is that everyone is laughing for no reason). Started by an Indian physician, Dr. Madan Kataria, in 1995, today there are more than six thousand "Social Laughter Clubs" in about sixty countries.

And speaking of doctors, here's one worth sharing.

Patient: "Doctor, you gotta help me. I'm under a lot of stress. I keep losing my temper with people."

Doctor: "Well, tell me about your problem."

Patient: "I just did, you friggin' imbecile!"

Based on the astounding range of physical, mental, and emotional health benefits of both the preventive and the curative kind, I very much hope that doctors will start to prescribe laughter to their patients. I hope they will recommend all of the positive Intense Experiences in this book to their patients, actually, but especially laughter. "Be sure to find a reason to laugh at least once every twenty minutes," they could advise, and I'd bet that our collective health would improve, along with driving down health-care costs tremendously. For that matter, particularly because laughter reduces stress, decreases anger, and alleviates other emotional issues while enhancing brainpower, wouldn't the intentional promotion of its use within schools make sense, especially in schools that face high levels of apathy and violence? What about in prisons and even in hostile territories at war or on the brink of it? Drop Ellen DeGeneres and Jay Leno on them instead of bombs.

There is always a time and a place for laughter, and that place and time are here and now. When things get especially challenging or overwhelmingly serious, that is when you should escalate the laughter. As long as you're not laughing at someone else and hurting the person's feelings—which is a form of anger, jealousy, and vengeance—laughter is nothing but gloriously beneficial and sorely needed.

But again, don't merely agree in theory with my words and all of the research on laughter. Immerse yourself in the following exercises to experience it, to live it and make it your own. Ideally, concentrate on doing these exercises for the next couple of weeks to really experience a remarkable uplift in your perspective, energy, health, and productivity and an amazing elimination of stress, loneliness, sadness, and feeling as if you want to punch somebody's nose. At least, immerse yourself in more of these exercises than you are doing today. As always, it is best to record what you experience in your journal or on paper, because that will make you deeply aware of the power of laughter so that you make it a habit to laugh more each day—at least 283 times more.

Five Intense Questions for You

1. Do you think you laugh enough? How many times can you recall laughing yesterday?

2. What are the two or three most embarrassing things that ever happened to you? Can you laugh about them and share them with others today? Sharing our most embarrassing stories is a great way to bond with others, because it acknowledges that we know we're human and don't take ourselves too seriously.

3. What topics tend to make you uncomfortable when people start to crack jokes about them? This can be a powerful way to discover hidden issues you may not have dealt with that are holding you down. Think about it.

4. Can you remember two or three situations in your life when you laughed so hard it hurt? Periodically revisit these stories whenever you need to laugh.

5. If you were a comedian using your own personal challenges and insecurities as your material, what would you mostly be making jokes about?

Laugh It Off Exercises

Exercise 1: Talk Stupid, Act Like an Idiot

I'll bet you never expected to find this advice in a book that will likely be shelved in the Self-Help section. Dress up in the most ridiculous and mismatched clothes you can find. Glop lipstick and other makeup all over your face. Grab the gel or the mousse, and create a beautiful mess on your head. Then go jump on your bed or on the trampoline in your neighbor's yard, and sing your favorite songs at the top of your lungs, while slurring all of the words. Have your significant other, friend, coworker, or coworker's significant other join you, if you want. Or at least parade around your house in your underwear, banging pots and pans with a spatula while singing "MacArthur Park" ("Someone left the cake out in the rain . . ."). This exercise is especially recommended if you are a bank executive, a U.S. senator, an angry talk show host, or someone who would never think of doing something like this.

Of course, you don't have to follow these particular suggestions. The point is to do something totally outside the realm of how you might spend a typical morning or evening and totally in the realm of the idiotic and ridiculous, so that you can laugh at yourself and remind your soul that although things may be serious, for crying out loud you're only human, and you're wearing a bra on your head, and things are never *that* serious as long as you can do this!

Many people are so stressed out, down on themselves, overwhelmed, apathetic, and feeling lost and lonely and angry because they see everything with such serious, gloom-and-doom eyes. Of course it's a vicious circle, because this morbid perspective breeds the negative emotions that produce more of the glum outlook, and so on. Step back to see how ridiculously funny the world can be, and jump in to see how absurd you can be. These are some of the strongest antidotes ever to gloom and doom.

To keep the world from getting you down, and when something already has you down, run around your house naked except for boots on your feet and earmuffs on your head and cackle like a chicken, or, if you're bold enough and the police aren't in the vicinity, do this or something just as ridiculous out in your yard. It's a powerful way not to take life too seriously and to gain a healthier perspective on whatever's got you down. Yes, it sounds zany. But really, what isn't?

Exercise 2: Collect the Funniest People You Know

Who are the funniest people you know? The friends, the coworkers, your family, your neighbors, and the coffee shop baristas who really make you laugh? Gather them up and keep them in a cage in your house so that you always have people near you who make you laugh. Feed them their favorite foods to make them even happier. If all of that seems a bit extreme, then jot down a list of all of the funniest people you know and make a point of going out to lunch or dinner with them, having them over to your house, and generally communicating with them much more often. Think about it: if laughter is the best medicine, then the people in your life who make you laugh are all your best doctors. So, be sure to play doctor with them as much as possible! Or at least head out for coffee or a cocktail with them far more than you currently do. And when you meet anyone new who makes you laugh, don't let the Prozac opportunity go. Befriend them, too, because you can never have enough funny docs in your life.

Exercise 3: Hunt Down *Ha!*

If corporations were really smart, they'd mandate that every day employees spend at least fifteen minutes reading, watching, and sharing funny stuff, both online and offline. I'd be willing to bet every cent of their profits that this would greatly increase employee morale, teamwork, creativity, problem-solving skills, and productivity—certainly far more than free doughnuts in the break room or that memo on corporate policy regarding staple-remover use. You may as well be an innovative leader and do this on your own.

Every day when you are in the thick of it, take breaks to find jokes online or read things that you've tucked into your purse or briefcase that make you laugh. The most important part of that last sentence is "when you are in the thick of it"; during the periods in your day when you have visions of your boss and coworkers trapped in a pit of venomous snakes and you're staring down at them and liking it, stop what you are doing. Head to the restroom and make a few ridiculous faces at yourself in the mirror. Then go online and find funny stuff. Watch YouTube videos. Google "funny pictures" and "funny cartoons" to experience an endless treasure chest of ha! Or if your company hasn't adopted the funny time policy yet and you're worried about being online, barricade yourself behind a restroom stall and crack open one of the hilarious books recommended further on in this chapter.

Make time every day, especially during the lowest points of the day, to find new things to laugh at. Whether it is videos, one-liners, pictures, or funny quotes, keep a collection of all of your favorites. I'm not kidding when I strongly suggest that you share these favorites not only with people you really like, to spread the cheer, but also with those who grate on your nerves—people you often envision in a venomous snake pit. Print out your favorite jokes and hand a copy to them, saying, "I am just sharing this with friends around me to brighten their day," or something like that. Sharing laughter softens, uplifts, and bonds people. It is mighty difficult to remain at odds with someone when you are laughing heartily together.

Exercise 4: Laugh at Starving Comedians

Aside from a world-class music concert, I've never felt so inspired and centered as during and after an exceptional live comedy show. Of course, most of them are not exceptional, but even the merely good comedy shows are great for blowing away those ashes and busting through rust and crust to make me feel much clearer and more energetic, creative, and motivated than when I walked in.

If you've never gone to a comedy show, try it. If you haven't done it in a while, try it again. I'd bet your next paycheck that you will find it a better investment of your time and money than spending another night in front of the tube eating stale crackers.

Go to comedy improvisation shows. Go see the local comedians in your area. If you've got no comedy venues nearby, it is well worth a trip to the nearest city. Or, at least, go to your local tavern and watch that guy who is always there and thinks he's a comedian. Maybe he actually is kind of funny, at least when he does that ape impression, at least after you've had a beer or two.

Beyond the fact that the comedians are funny, it is the experience of laughing with a bunch of other people who are laughing that makes live comedy and improvisation shows so uniquely uplifting. Research shows that people laugh about thirty times more in social situations than they do when they are alone. As you already realize, if you've ever paid attention to sitcoms on TV where they edit in canned laughter, hearing other people laughing is contagious. It actually makes whatever you experience even funnier when others laugh at it. In other words, you are going to laugh your ashes off in a big way at even merely good live comedy shows, perhaps considerably more than you would if you were alone watching that same comedy show on TV. That's kind of like knowing you can take a hot shower alone and feel good, but if you take that same hot shower with a bunch of other people, you will feel thirty times better. Which would you choose? Okay, maybe it's not exactly like that, but you get the idea. The shared experience of the laughter is the thing.

That said, even if you cannot get out of the house, watching comedians on TV or YouTube is still a mighty therapeutic experience. Invite family, friends, and the coffee shop barista over to watch comedy with you to make it even healthier.

Exercise 5: All Right, Watch TV

For this one exercise only, I am going to encourage you to watch some TV. Because one of the areas in which TV can be beneficial— if you are aware of it, versus getting sucked into it—is in making you laugh. Some of the funniest stuff ever created anywhere, in fact, has been made for TV.

First, make a list of your all-time-favorite funniest shows on TV, from your childhood through today. Some of these are available on cable TV, and you can find collections of your funniest TV shows in video stores and online.

Also use this opportunity to explore other funny shows that you may never have seen before. Following are some shows often cited in various lists as the funniest; try to watch the ones you haven't seen before, and ask other people for their recommendations.

Funniest TV Shows
All in the Family
The Andy Griffith Show
The Carol Burnett Show
Cheers
The Colbert Report
The Cosby Show
Curb Your Enthusiasm
The Daily Show with Jon Stewart
David Letterman
Family Ties
Frasier
Friends
Happy Days
The Honeymooners
I Love Lucy
The Jeffersons
Laverne & Shirley
M.A.S.H.
Monty Python's Flying Circus
The Office
Roseanne
Sanford and Son
Saturday Night Live

SCTV
Seinfeld
The Simpsons
Soap
South Park
Taxi
The Tonight Show
Three's Company
The Wonder Years
Welcome Back, Kotter
WKRP in Cincinnati

In addition, also watch as many of the funniest films of all time as you can fit into your schedule. These will include your own personal favorites, the following recommendations, and suggestions you find elsewhere.

Funniest Movies
Airplane!
Animal House
Annie Hall
Big
The Big Lebowski
Blazing Saddles
Caddyshack
Clerks
Coming to America
Dr. Strangelove
Dumb and Dumber
Fast Times at Ridgemont High
Ferris Bueller's Day Off

A Fish Called Wanda
The 40-Year-Old Virgin
Groundhog Day
The Hangover
I'm Gonna Git You, Sucka
Knocked Up
Meet the Fockers
Modern Times
Monty Python and the Holy Grail
My Big Fat Greek Wedding
Naked Gun
National Lampoon's Vacation
The Pink Panther
Planes, Trains and Automobiles
Raising Arizona
Spaceballs
Stripes
Superbad
There's Something about Mary
This Is Spinal Tap
Wedding Crashers
The Wedding Singer

Exercise 6: Read This Stuff in the Restroom

I got news for you—if it wasn't for the toilet, there would be no books!

—*George Costanza on* Seinfeld

In 1991, a small publisher released a book called *Compact Classics* that summarized and condensed various works of great literature down to two pages each. It didn't sell much. But when it was renamed *The Great American Bathroom Book*, it went on to sell more than a million copies. I think so many people enjoy reading in the restroom at home and at work because there is relatively little chance of being disturbed there, it's generally pretty quiet, and it's a rather warm and comfortable seat. I find it particularly enjoyable to read humorous material in the restroom, perhaps because it synchronizes so well with the humbling human truth of what typically takes place there. Am I being too subtle?

No matter where you like to read, during the next week or two as you focus on Laughing It Off, shelve as much of the other stuff you may be reading and dive instead into all of the funny things you can get your hands on.

Read the comics in the *New Yorker*, at Salon.com, and in your local newspaper. Instead of surfing the Internet yet again to discover another disease whose symptoms sound like something you might have, head to TheOnion.com for its brilliant satire. A few other online favorites include BorowitzReport.com, BongoNews.com, Funny-Stuff-Central.com, and ModernHumorist.com. Go to FunnyTimes.com, and get yourself a subscription to this hilarious monthly newspaper that will make you excited about receiving snail mail again.

And pick up a humorous book or two and read those. It's hard not to love anything by Erma Bombeck, Dave Barry, David Sedaris, Bill Bryson, and Douglas Adams. Following are some of my own personal recommendations.

> *Bridget Jones's Diary,* **Helen Fielding.** If you're a woman, read it. If you're a man who interacts with women, read it. If you're not, read it.
>
> *A Dirty Job,* **Christopher Moore.** Pick up this book by one of today's most consistently funny writers, look Death in the face, and laugh hard.
>
> *Good Omens: The Nice and Accurate Prophecies of Agnes Nutter, Witch,* **Terry Pratchett and Neil Gaiman.** These

two writers have created some comedic wonders of their own, Pratchett's edging toward exceptional silliness and Gaiman's toward morbid laughs. Together, they have created one of the greatest satires I've read in years.

Right Ho, Jeeves! **P. G. Wodehouse.** P. G. Wodehouse's entire series of books featuring the valet and "gentleman's personal gentleman" Reginald Jeeves are among the funniest things ever written, and this one is the best. If you enjoy Monty Python and British humor especially, don't miss it.

Things My Girlfriend and I Have Argued About, **Mil Millington.** An ex-girlfriend of mine and I once had an argument about whether Vanilla Ice's song "Ice, Ice Baby" should be played at parties. We finally laughed about the argument, but only after several hours of serious heat. Mil Millington has written a hilarious book whose title says exactly what it is about—and then some. Certain people may find themselves in tears of laughter while reading this one.

Exercise 7: Laugh Even If Nothing Is Funny

Go ahead right now and laugh. I'm not even going to tell you a joke. Just go ahead and belt out a good fake laugh. Come on, give it your best shot!

Earlier in this experience, I mentioned that even feigning laughter can provide you with immense benefits. That's because laughter releases endorphins that make you feel good, relaxes your muscles, suppresses the mean hormones that make you feel stressed, and more.

During the course of this experience—and, like everything else in this book, hopefully for the rest of your life—make it a habit to laugh every time you look in the mirror. It's a great way to start the day, it's fun to do anytime you look in the mirror during the day (if you're vain, you'll be laughing a lot!), and it's a terrific way to end the day. Some people have found it helpful to write the word "Laugh!" (or any funny word that will remind you to laugh and might make others wonder, such as "Flump") on sticky notes and place them on the mirror, the car dashboard, and anywhere they'll see the word during the course of the day.

You can take one giant scissor-step forward and find a Laughter Club in your area (do a Google search for "Laughter Club" and the name of your area—easy, right?). As you already know, laughing with others—even if it starts off as fake laughing—makes the experience far more enjoyable and healthy. After you've gone to a few sessions, though, here's a challenge for you: while everyone around you is laughing their ashes off, try hard to keep a straight face. I'll bet your entire retirement savings account that you can't!

Exercise 8: Host Macaroni, Chili, and Underwear Parties

Imagine hosting a party where everyone who is invited brings his or her favorite jokes, short stories, one-liners, limericks, humorous news stories, funny songs, funny quotes, and cartoon clippings to pass around for everyone else.

Imagine having a party where everyone dresses in a ridiculous theme, such as their favorite fruit or vegetable or as punk rock Puritans or in their underwear, if you dare.

Imagine, after sharing the jokes, that everyone also shares a true story of the funniest or most embarrassing thing that ever happened to him or her.

Imagine having people each sing a karaoke song of their choice at the party in their best falsetto voices; playing funny games such as Balderdash, Pictionary, Scruples, and Twister; and requiring everyone to eat macaroni and chili for dinner and cake for dessert with absolutely no utensils.

Then make it happen. Make it a yearly or quarterly tradition. In addition to laughing harder than you may have ever laughed in your life and providing people with memories that will have them laughing for the rest of their lives, everyone will love you and erect bronze statues of you in their front yards.

Have mini-versions of these funny parties at your cubicle at work, too. Just check the corporate dress code first if you'll be encouraging your work mates to attend your little soiree in their underwear.

Exercise 9: Seek the LOL in Every Situation

So you've lost your job, home, and car, and the only things you still own are the clothes on your back and a Foreman grill. Your spouse ran off with your marriage counselor, all of your so-called best friends are standing up in their wedding, and you just discovered that even your dog hasn't been faithful to you. Find the humor in it! Laugh about it!

Okay, it's far easier said than done. But when you're down, one of the healthiest and most important things you can do is surround yourself with plenty of up. Because you are down, naturally it can be very difficult on your own to seek the Ha! in every situation. If you could, obviously you wouldn't be so down.

That is why it is so important to bring far more of the experience of laughter into your life, starting now. It's like taking vitamin C. Get plenty of vitamin C routinely in your diet, and you'll ward off some attacks of flu and colds altogether, and those that do strike won't hit you as hard. When you do feel them coming on, escalate your intake of vitamin C to alleviate their impact even more. Similarly, start with the exercises in this chapter to make laughing hundreds of times per day a habit again, as you did when you were a child, and you'll avoid sinking nearly as low as you'd otherwise go when life throws dogs that cheat on you your way. When you feel low, surround yourself with things of joy and laughter. It is not the total solution, of course—conversation with family and friends, finding peace and perspective in nature (such as talking to your tree), getting professional help, creating a kick-butt résumé and sending it out in droves, and other measures are also essential. But immersing yourself in experiences that have the potential to make you smile and laugh when you are down is a key part of the solution, because it can only add light to your perspective.

If you can routinely smile and laugh a whole lot more than you do today—mirth is one thing that violates the "Everything in moderation" rule—you will ward off plenty of darkness, and you'll also learn to welcome even more smiles and laughter when the darkness creeps in anyway. By doing this, you will be far better equipped to see the Ha! in every challenging situation, which in turn helps you better deal with it.

Then you'll be able to see the shedding of your job, home, car, spouse, best friends, and dog not as a tragic loss, but as God and the universe sending you a message that now is a time of rebirth, a time of wide-open possibilities, a time to blaze new trails, a time to get a new and better breed of dog, and a time to finally discover all of those different ways of using your Foreman grill that are described in the instructions.

Intense Experience #6

✺

Reveal Yourself

Fear makes strangers of people who would be friends.
—*Shirley Maclaine*

Remember that everyone you meet is afraid of something, loves something, and has lost something.
—*H. Jackson Brown Jr.*

The secret to a rich life is to have more beginnings than endings.
—*David Weinbaum*

I n my early twenties, I was a full-time student at Northern Illinois University (NIU). I also worked nearly full-time at a number of jobs. And I was a full-time married father of a baby. Although my wife and I were committed parents who enjoyed the experience of raising our boy, I was lonely, sad, and angry. Still basically a child myself, I was an undergraduate among other undergraduates in the place—college—that doubles as a scholarly institution and an amusement park. But for me, there was no dorm or fraternity life, no freedom to date around, wander into fun and foolish places on nights and weekends, and make mistakes with merely short-term consequences. For me, the same mistakes would mean much greater consequences. If it were not for a certain stranger, I am not sure I would have made it through college at all.

I usually studied at night at a restaurant, and that's where I met Jeff Davis. One of us struck up a conversation—about Michael Jordan's game the night before, I believe—and our discussion progressed to perhaps my most important discovery at NIU: Jeff, who is a year younger than me, was also a full-time student who was working nearly full-time. And he was married. And he and his wife had a baby they were raising. As we became good friends, I discovered that Jeff was experiencing the same emotions that only someone in those circumstances could really understand. The conversations we had, the fun we had, and the support we provided to each other carried us both through. Today Jeff lives several hours away, and we see each other only periodically, but he is one of those friends with whom, no matter how much time goes by, things pick up exactly where they left off. Our friendship wouldn't have existed, and my life would be the worse for it, if two strangers had not struck up a conversation in a restaurant.

Consider your life. Consider the difficult phases where you somehow made it through, your grandest successes so far, and the greatest times of joy you've ever experienced. Notice how there was always someone else, if not multiple people, who helped you in each of those situations. Even if the greatest joy you ever experienced was a year alone on a mountaintop, there are people in your life who deserve credit for helping you get there. It is inevitable. And they were all once strangers to you.

Every teacher, friend, and person whose words or deeds helped you in some way, great or small, and every family member—even your mother when you were born—was once a stranger to you. In every circumstance, there came a moment of transition, when you and this person who had never before seen or acknowledged each other made your introductions. "Hi, how are you?" "Welcome to the world, baby." "How about Jordan's game last night?" It is true that some of these meetings were passive—you had no choice but to meet your mother—but many of the most meaningful acquaintances in your life happened because someone took the initiative.

In every situation where one stranger is in your vicinity, there is at the least a chance to exchange warmth and laughter, and that is so worthwhile. In every situation where fifteen strangers are in your vicinity, there is at least one person who can make a significant impact on your life. In any situation where forty strangers are in your vicinity, there is at least one person who can change your life in profoundly positive ways. Those are not scientifically accurate numbers, but I know I am being conservative.

Grab All of the Toys You Want

It is like that ducky game at the carnival, where those cute little plastic ducks are floating around in a circle, and your mission is simply to reach out and pick one up. Every duck is a winner. On the bottom of the duck is a number indicating your prize, and although most of the time you're only going to get a little prize like a Super Ball, sometimes you get the big prize, like the giant stuffed Scooby-Doo.

Yet with so many ducks circling around out there in life—and you don't even need a dollar to play—most adults stop reaching for them. People lament the relationships they don't have, the jobs they don't love, the issues they are facing, and more, but even though many of those ducks contain a prize that most certainly could help the people, they're not reaching for the ducks.

Instead, they have locked themselves inside, away from the carnival. They've barricaded themselves within the walls of their homes, cars, offices, and cubicles; within shopping malls and the bland repetitive boxes of chain stores and restaurants that have infested the American landscape. Within these walls, they've barricaded themselves into the even tighter walls of their computer screens, cell phone screens, TV screens, and other screens. We've already covered the impact of this in previous Intense Experiences; people now spend 90 percent of their lives indoors, and the lack of being out in nature has devastating consequences. Overworking is rampant, and when people aren't working, they're shopping, surfing the Web, watching TV for 153 hours per month, and spending more than 100 hours a year just commuting to work, all of which has had devastating consequences on the depth of communication within families and has led to a loneliness epidemic. To top it off, what people are consuming from the TV, the Internet, grocery stores, and all of the rest is largely mediocre, heaping insult onto injury.

As covered in the Dive Deeper into Your Blood experience, people are not even communicating in depth in their existing relationships, much less reaching out to meet strangers. Because people have locked themselves inside bland places, it really shouldn't be surprising that they feel locked up and bland inside.

The main intent of the following exercises is for you to experience how, by exposing yourself to more people, you'll inevitably open doors in your career, finances, love and spirit, and overall success and happiness. Some of the exercises also require exposing yourself to strange new things. That's really what this entire book encourages you to do, but as you are consciously changing your habits and encountering more human strangers during the next few weeks, it is a particularly powerful time to go where you haven't gone before in other areas, too. Doing the two simultaneously— meeting human strangers and going beyond your comfort zone by trying new foods and so on—escalates the power and impact of each one. As always, the main idea is to allow you to discover first-hand, by doing versus merely reading about, why you will want to commit to meeting more strangers of both the human and non-human variety for the rest of your life.

Now go reach for those ducks—you can pick as many as you want.

Five Intense Questions for You

1. Who is the most unusual person you've ever befriended, whose eccentric manner, choices, background, or other traits made him or her a type of person you never expected to befriend?

2. Which friends and acquaintances from the past would you most like to reconnect with, whether for personal reasons, business possibilities, or both?

3. Take a step-by-step mind tour of a typical weekday and a typical weekend day in your life. How many opportunities to meet new people are already present, whether at coffee shops, in the workplace, on trains or buses, or elsewhere? How can you increase these opportunities?

4. Who are three acquaintances or complete strangers you encounter occasionally or routinely whom you believe would be most likely to become friends of yours? Think of people you correspond with through work, in stores and restaurants, while traveling, and beyond.

5. Do you find it easy to meet new people and make new friends? Or do you tend to close off to meeting new people? Why do you believe that is so?

Reveal Yourself Exercises

Exercise 1: Meet Strangers without Really Meeting Strangers

Creative visualization is the practice of achieving peak performance in a situation in the outside world by first picturing it in your mind. Athletes often use this technique; for example, some golfers play through holes on a certain course repeatedly in their minds before they ever step onto the actual course. They watch their hands hold the club and take aim, feel themselves swing and connect properly, and watch the ball drop into the hole. Various studies have demonstrated the efficacy of creative visualization, including a famous one that showed that Olympic athletes who incorporated this mental training into their lives outperformed those who did not, and the more they did incorporate it, the more they outperformed athletes who did not.

Because the idea of approaching strangers simply to say hello and strike up a conversation is foreign to many people and even provokes anxiety in some, and because even those who feel comfortable enough doing it can only polish their methods and accelerate making it a habit, I want you to visualize meeting strangers in your mind.

Find a quiet place where you can relax your mind and body. Close your eyes. Visualize some place that you frequent where there are often other people around whom you don't really know, such as your workplace, a coffee shop, a restaurant, a church, or the airport. Through your own eyes and other senses—in the first person, that is, not as if you were outside of yourself—notice the details of the place as much as possible in your mind, such as its furniture and colors, the typical sounds and smells of the place, how the door feels as you enter, and so on, until you are "there." If strangers are often present in whatever place you've gone to, such as work mates you have never talked to before, picture those people. If it is a place where you rarely see the same person twice, let your mind simply invent the strangers around you. (It is amazing how the mind can actually "invent" strangers, with their unique facial features, the clothes they are wearing, and more, as if they were real people. Perhaps this is your brain retaining memories of actual people you once passed near but never really noticed, or it may be an amalgamation of different people.) Then choose a person you want to approach, whether it's because he or she is standing in front of you in line, because you think the person is cute or looks interesting, or whatever your reason.

Notice how you feel at this point. Are you nervous? Are thoughts entering your mind, such as, What if he thinks I am crazy? or What if she just ignores me? Separately from this visualization, it may be worthwhile to explore where those fears and doubts stem from, with the goal of eliminating the blocks inside you, but right now, feel the fear and the doubt yet stay determined on your path of doing it anyway. What are you going to say to this stranger by way of introduction? Let me stress right now—don't overthink this. If you are going to err, do so in the direction of underthinking what you will say. The simple "How about this weather?" can open doors as well as anything can, because after a bit of banter about how cold or hot it is, it's easy to ask something like, "So, you live in this area?" or "What type of work do you do?" I've also found that giving a compliment about something a person is wearing helps a stranger open up. It could be a piece of jewelry: "Those are beautiful earrings, where'd you get them?" or someone's car—"What do you think of that Dodge Viper, overall?" So, now in your visualization, perhaps find something of a stranger's to compliment. Then play both sides of the conversation for a bit. Keep the conversation flowing, as you ask questions and answer them for both sides. You don't really know how a stranger would respond to where she got her earrings, of course, but the point here is just to practice getting comfortable with enabling the conversation to flow. When tennis players use creative visualization, they're similarly seeing and feeling the game through their own eyes, in first person, but they're also playing their opponent's game, because their main intent is to practice performing optimally, no matter what their opponent does.

Because we do live in a society of walled-in people, don't be surprised when in person you really do encounter some people who act as if you intend to bite them just because you say hello and strike up a conversation. They'll initially suspect that you are up to something, like trying to lure them into your cult. Visualize this type of scenario, too, and how you would put them at ease or finally back politely away if they were just too stiff and scared.

Although creative visualization may be brand new to you, try it. It works because it's sort of a trick to your brain, which doesn't know the difference between what "really" happened versus what you visualized happening; the input it is receiving is the same. You are getting experience and become smoother at it simply by visualizing. The more the idea of approaching strangers makes you nervous or anxious, the more you may want to practice visualizations of it. You may become more interested in harnessing the benefits of creative visualization in other areas of your life, too. If so, I recommend the book *Creative Visualization: Use the Power of Your Imagination to Create What You Want in Life* by Shakti Gawain.

Exercise 2: Strike Gold at Least Once a Week

If you knew that by digging twenty-five holes per week, you'd strike gold that would make you wealthier at least once a week, would you do it? Well, by initiating conversation with twenty-five strangers each week, you are guaranteed to strike gold at least once a week. Why wouldn't you do it?

Here are just a few examples of what someone who is currently a stranger might actually become in your life: the missing link to a better job; someone who has gone through or is going through similar challenges that you are facing, who can lend valuable insight and support; someone who shares your hobbies; someone who needs whatever it is you may sell; someone who can fix your broken ceiling fan or do your taxes; or someone who has children your children's age, who are ideal for playdates. He or she might be a new best friend or your future spouse. Every romantic relationship and lifelong marriage started out between two strangers, after all.

For the next week or two, experience it for yourself. Strike up a conversation with at least twenty-five people per week. Break it down into five people per day or whatever variation works best for you. If you work in a big company among many strangers, it is easy to start there. It is quite odd that people see so many of the same people, day in and day out, on the elevator and in cubicles on the other side of the building, who may hold the key to a happier life in ways small or large, and yet they remain strange faces. Of course, there are endless opportunities to meet strangers elsewhere, too: in stores, in restaurants, at the post office, walking through your neighborhood, and so on. You can use the random approach and target anyone in your vicinity; you'll strike gold. If you are single and looking, feel the fear of rejection and do it anyway—rejection means you are moving forward—and target the men or the women who catch your eye. Eventually, you will again strike gold, and you may enjoy some silver, bronze, or, at least, aluminum along the way to finding your gold. Or simply rely on your intuition. If you open yourself up to your sixth sense, you will come to notice that although many people are indeed afraid of others and may take a bit more work on your part, many others will glow with welcome when you introduce yourself.

Exercise 3: Let the Wise Owls and Pups Feed You

During the next several weeks, befriend three or more people who are at least twenty years older than you. If you're in your twenties to fifties, aim for at least thirty-five years older than you—the "old people."

Also within the next several weeks, if you are around your mid-thirties or beyond, try to befriend three or more people who are at least fifteen to twenty years younger than you. If you are in your fifties or beyond, try for those who are at least thirty years younger than you.

According to a 2009 study by the Pew Research Center, there is a very wide generational gap today—nearly as strong as it was in the 1960s, although it is considerably more subdued now compared to then. Seventy-nine percent of all Americans say there are major differences in the points of view of younger versus older adults. This includes differences in terms of work ethic, moral values, the respect people show others, attitudes about different races and groups, and religious views. Interestingly, by great margins even among the young, the perception is that older Americans are superior in their work ethic, their moral values, and the respect they show others. Meanwhile, the majority of both young and old believe that younger people are superior when it comes to accepting different races and groups.

These differences are not a cause to hide within the comfort of your age group. There is no growth in hiding. The differences instead point to a golden opportunity to leap across those generational lines and really listen to and engage with those who are considerably younger and older. I assure you that you'll discover myriad benefits in doing so; the wider your circle of friends outside your age-related comfort range and the deeper your conversations with them, the more benefits you will find.

Profound wisdom can come with age and experience. Yet being "old" doesn't automatically qualify someone as being wise; there are plenty of people who after many decades still haven't worked at becoming aware of or clear of the rust and the crust inside them that blocks them from experiencing deep knowledge and inner peace. Bitter old fools are as prevalent as reckless young fools, and while they deserve our compassion and attention, and there is always something worth learning from anyone, they're not going to be fountains of wisdom. Those who are aware and dedicated, however, and who have lived through many decades of Intense Experiences tend to be the wisest of all.

Although a wise owl may not be best qualified to recommend the latest and greatest new technology or music, in terms of what matters most and makes life worth living—love, kindness, commitment, self-awareness—experience really is the best teacher when the student is a dedicated student. The gifts a wise owl can give you in this regard, if you are open to receiving them, are among the most valuable gifts available to you anywhere.

Befriend at least three wise owls. If you are really committed to bettering your own life, head to retirement communities and nursing homes and volunteer to engage with people there. Again, you will encounter some old fools and also people who simply because of health issues cannot function well anymore, but you will inevitably find your wise owls.

Meanwhile, youth and its innocence are their own form of wisdom. With age and experience, so much important knowledge can be gained, but so often many other crucial types of knowledge are lost in the process. Hope, perseverance, awe, and unrelenting joy are common among these losses. With the experience of getting burned, one can learn to be cautious when dancing too close to the flames, but then so many people stop dancing altogether. Befriend at least three wise pups. You may have to encounter angry or apathetic pups en route to finding three wise ones, but the raw wisdom and the energy the wise pups will radiate are well worth it.

Exercise 4: Allow Strangers to Reveal Themselves to You

Journey further outside your comfort zone to continue clearing through your rust and crust so that you can become as happy and successful as you know you were meant to be.

First, grab your journal and a pen, go to a place of solitude, and make an honest list of all of the different "types" of people you hold grudges against, fear, or have some form of prejudice against. This can be a difficult exercise at first, because not being prejudiced has been trumpeted so loudly in recent decades that you may not want to believe you could possibly have prejudices. It is "bad." It might make you ashamed to discover that you do have prejudices, so it is easier not to even go there. But it is nothing to be ashamed of; if you are willing to honestly recognize and confront your prejudices, this is in fact quite good. It eliminates a blockage from the world and a blockage inside you.

First, make that list. Are gay people on your list? Or straight people, if you are gay? People of another race? From different countries? People who believe in other religions or atheists? People who work in blue-collar jobs, white-collar jobs, or any specific type of jobs? Pop singers, country musicians, rappers? Those who live in the suburbs, in rural areas, or the city? Jocks, scholars, artists, businesspeople, the homeless? Liberals, conservatives?

It is likely that you are making assumptions about, and passing judgment on, some people grouped within some area. Again, unless you intentionally act in hateful ways toward that group, this is nothing to be ashamed about. It is instead something to understand so that you can work toward eliminating it. This way, you, and all of us, can grow. No one is only liberal, conservative, gay, straight, black, white, French, American, or a street sweeper or a stockbroker. Those terms are only some of nearly infinite labels that people, like you, wear. So, when you have made your list, question why you hold the prejudice. Understand what you may fear or what beliefs may have been handed down to you by others, such as parents, clergy, the media, or the like. Discover the cause in order to cure prejudice in yourself.

If you are experiencing stubborn blocks on this front, think about a best friend or someone you dearly love. Now imagine that this person announces to you that he or she is entering one of those groups you hold a prejudice against. Or that this person or someone he or she dearly loves is marrying someone from one of those groups. Would you disown the person? It may make you uncomfortable initially, and you might be tempted to pass judgment on the person at first, but, hopefully, you would ultimately seek to understand him or her, based on your love and friendship.

There are always exceptions, I realize, and I also understand that what is not an exception to one person will always be to another. If you are prejudiced against members of a violent gang, well, that makes perfect sense. Me, too. But I realize, for example, that some pro-lifers believe that pro-choicers are members of a violent gang, and vice versa. As long as there is freedom of thought, some prejudices will always remain. Yet as we've witnessed here in the United States, in the last fifty years especially, many prejudices can be reduced and eliminated, and I believe that most will be. Individually and collectively, we're each and all better for it.

After you finish your list, make it a point—with an open and loving heart—to meet strangers within each of your prejudice areas. Talk with them and befriend them. Use creative visualization to walk through doing so, as necessary. Unless you live in an area that is very rich in diversity, you won't be able to accomplish this in the next few weeks or even months. Consider making it a lifelong mission—to befriend at least one person in every group you hold a prejudice against. That one person can break down your prejudice altogether, opening doors to many more people who hold the potential of providing greater meaning and happiness in your own life. Think about it. This may be among the most difficult exercises in the entire book, but I can assure you that it is also among the most rewarding.

Exercise 5: Be a Groupie

A study of 4,725 random residents of Alameda County, California, demonstrated that those with the fewest social connections had mortality rates that were two to three times higher than the death rates of people with strong social ties. I discussed the loneliness epidemic in more depth in the Dive Deeper into Your Blood experience, but this is worth repeating: not only does feeling lonely inhibit your success, inner peace, and happiness, but it is clearly associated with diseases such as cancer, respiratory and gastrointestinal illnesses, heart disease, and early death.

Get out of the house, get away from the office, leave the comfortable quarters of your existing circle of acquaintances, and go meet new people! If any of the previous exercises left you muttering something like, "But I don't get out much to meet new people in the first place," then this is especially true for you.

During the next few weeks, commit to attending at least three groups or social events in your community that you've never attended before. They can center on networking with other people in your community, such as the Jaycees, the Elks Club, or the Rotary Club. They may focus on activist or community causes, religion, sports, hobbies, or the arts. If you are in the United States, go to www.MeetUp.com, where you will find groups united around everything and anything you can imagine (and plenty you cannot) there in your area.

Make it a point to meet new people at these meetings; you can easily reach your weekly goal of turning twenty-five strangers into acquaintances and friends by attending these meetings alone. Furthermore, these groups and meetings may expose you to ideas, interests, and creative outlets that were once strange to you as well, which is rewarding in and of itself.

Exercise 6: Indulge in Fried Insects

In Bangkok, Thailand, fried water bugs, silkworms, grasshoppers, and crickets are popular snacks from street vendors. I hear they taste more like seafood than chicken. I haven't been to Thailand yet, but I envision that when I go I'll stand before a cart loaded with these once-squirming and now crunchy critters, squirming myself as I debate whether I should try one. Perhaps unless I first decide to sample Thailand's popular *lâo khão*, or "white liquor," which is made from sticky rice and contains 35 percent alcohol, I think my stomach will tell me, "No way, you are not eating a bug, Brian." Everyone has his limitations, and some with good reason.

That said—and now that I've got your mouth watering—I encourage you, as you intentionally open doors with new people, to also open doors to new foods you haven't tried before. And to delve into new genres of music, film, literature, and other arts and new sports, hobbies, destinations, and even fashions that have been a stranger to you. Doing so has been recommended elsewhere in this book, but here I urge you to first have fun making lists of things by category that you have never done or tried; for example, create headings like "Ethnic Foods I Haven't Tried," "Genres of Books I Haven't Read," "Sports Events I Haven't Attended," and then list your answers underneath each.

For decades, I criticized the music of Barry Manilow, largely because it is a guy thing to do. Then I married one of Barry's biggest fans, and I actually had to listen to his music. It wasn't Bach or U2, but I liked it. I would sing right along to "Time in New England" and all the rest with my wife in the car. When Barry came to Chicago in concert, it seemed like the perfect gift for my wife, and because she needed someone to go with, I figured I'd sacrifice myself. It turned out to be one of the most soulful and uplifting concerts I'd ever experienced. Even now, divorced, I confess I still listen to the occasional Barry Manilow song—intentionally.

With all of the infinite things that are a stranger to you, even those you always convinced yourself you were not interested in and wouldn't appreciate because you didn't like them when you were young or there is some social label associated with them, there are gifts waiting. Transformations small and large are waiting. You won't resonate with all of these strangers, but I can guarantee that you will with some. Jazz, romance novels, foreign films, Ethiopian food, ballet, maybe fried water bugs—step beyond your zone of familiarity, open your heart and mind, be patient at first, and allow them to help you grow.

Exercise 7: Befriend Those on Opposite Sides of Your World

When you really get to know people from foreign worlds—whether that means they're living lives drastically different from yours, such as soldiers or prisoners, or they're living in very differ-ent cultures—you will inevitably gain an amazing perspective on your own life.

Yet unless you can travel for weeks to a distant land, or you do something that lands you in prison, developing a pen-pal relation-ship is the most effective way to engage with these people. First of all, it is simply interesting and inspiring to discover how they live—how so much is different, but so much is the same. Plus, this is one of the most powerful but least utilized ways to remind yourself of what really matters in your own life, of all you have that is so worthwhile and what is worth—and not worth—invest-ing your energy in.

To develop pen-pal relationships with people you otherwise have no access to, just do a Google search for "penpals" and you'll discover multiple options, including the most popular: www .InterPals.net. Although a fair amount of international flirting is happening on that site to be aware of—or indulge in, if you choose—there are plenty of people from every country in the world seeking pen-pal friends there, too. InterPals.net has a great feature where you can search for a pen pal by country. In exchang-ing stories about what daily life is like, and the challenges and joys you each are facing, do not be surprised if you end up keeping some of these relationships for life. And do not be surprised if this eventually gives you a wonderful reason to travel to foreign worlds to meet your good friend.

Exercise 8: Get Lost

Throw some beverages and snacks in a bag, get in your car, and drive away. Keep your GPS and maps at home. Prepare to be gone at least the entire day; if you can stay away overnight, even bet-ter, and if you can make your trip last an entire week, better still. Just get in your car and drive away. If you would prefer a different mode of transportation, by all means use that. Have absolutely no destination in mind—it is important that you don't have any intention of ending up somewhere specifically. Start on the street in front of your home, and then follow your impulses as they lead you on. Turn onto roads and highways that strike your fancy. Get off on exit ramps that call out to you. Pay no attention to street names, highway markers, town names, or any labels whatsoever that indicate where you are. You are simply here. Just keep driving, taking turns onto roads that you want to explore, and drive some more. Get far outside your zone of familiarity. Go until you're somewhere you've never been before. Keep going if you want to. Get completely lost.

Once you are lost, but only when you are inspired to, park your car. If you are feeling fear, fine: that's just a doorway to walk through to the unknown and all of the gifts it holds in store. Of course, if you sense real danger—if there are beings walking around out there with blood on their fangs and they are eyeing you like steak—drive on. There are various types of fear, and you'll know the difference between one that is a doorway to walk through and another that is a warning to turn back. Trust yourself.

When you have stopped where you're meant to stop, be it a small town, a lake, a neighborhood, a flea market, or anywhere at all, go experience what your impulses tell you to experience. If you are in a small town, for example, wander into the restaurants, the shops, the nurseries, or wherever you are called to explore. Initiate conversations with strangers, asking them about themselves, their town, or whatever you want to bring up.

Wander in, and pay close attention to the environment around you: the trees, rocks on the shore, animals, books and knickknacks on the shelves, buildings, abandoned appliances, and so on. Especially pay attention to people, if they are present—strike up those conversations. Because, although in a conventional sense you are lost, you are exactly where you are meant to be. And there is at least one someone or one something of great value for you there. Perhaps an important thought contained inside you has been waiting for this particular situation to come out, to change your perspective or life. Perhaps a meaningful gift for you to give someone you love is sitting there on the dusty shelves of an antiques shop. Or maybe the man who will become your husband is walking right toward you on that path in a park. I cannot tell you specifically what you will find, but I can say that there are reasons you followed your impulses in getting lost and wandering where you did. Discover those reasons.

If you have more time on your journey, continue to follow your impulses. Stay in that place to wander farther into it and to meet still more people. Or drive some more, until you are compelled to stop somewhere else and wander into that place.

We live in a world where people worry so much about getting lost, about veering off the safe routes they know or that microchips tell them is the correct way to travel. The sure path is obviously a good thing sometimes; don't intentionally get lost if you need to be at work in an hour. But if you seek change in any area, the only way is to drive beyond the familiar, to drive through the fear until you are lost in the new, and to be aware of and relish what you encounter there. That is true both figuratively and literally.

I intentionally get lost often. I've worked on significant parts of this book in greasy spoons, coffee shops, and overpriced seafood restaurants in towns and neighborhoods I never saw before and may never again. I actually like to edit what I've already written in these new places because the new environment often lends me a different perspective that only enhances the work. Just yesterday, I wandered until I came upon the quaint downtown of a Chicago suburb I'd never been in and decided that was the place for me. Before sitting down to work in a coffee shop, I took a walk around and met a hair stylist who started a conversation with me. Within ten minutes, he was trying to set me up on dates with clients of his. Within twenty minutes of conversation, he gave me a $30 gift certificate for a haircut and a style. Not a monumental shift in my life, but still an unexpected gift. I am grateful, and it looks like I'll be heading back to that particular suburb! I've met people who became good friends, girlfriends, and business associates by getting lost. I've found inspiration, ideas, and direction by getting completely lost in forests and fields. In a small flea market somewhere in the middle of Michigan, I found a three-and-a-half-foot-tall armored knight—made by some creative soul from discarded metal—which has been guarding the doorway to my home now for years.

Where you end up when you get lost is exactly where you were meant to be. Strange lands are opportunities, and they hold at least one secret of worth to you. Be aware, because there is some reason you are there.

Get lost frequently. Get lost on day trips, overnights, and at least once in your life get lost on a weeklong trip where you book a flight somewhere that just calls out to you and, with no plans beyond that, you simply go and wander. Get lost alone. Get lost with a family member or a friend, which is an entirely different experience than doing so alone. Get lost to find more of yourself.

Then, with your newfound knowledge, no worries, and no GPS, find your way back home. There's no place like it, but after a journey like this, it will always be a different place, because, in ways small or large, you will have grown.

Intense Experience #7

෧

Give to *Really* Live

Those who bring sunshine into the lives of others cannot keep it from themselves.

—*James M. Barrie*

If you want to lift yourself up, lift up someone else.

—*Booker T. Washington*

Surely the earth can be saved by all the people who insist on love.

—*Alice Walker*

When news of the events of September 11, 2001, finally reached a group of Kenyan Masai herders, they responded by donating a gift that touched hearts throughout the world: they gave the United States fourteen highly prized cattle. By Western standards, these Masai are anything but wealthy, and the worth of one head of cattle—which are sacred to them—is immense. For these Masai, giving away fourteen is a remarkably generous gesture akin to you or me giving away a sizable chunk of our income that we could instead use to pay our bills.

Wilson Naiyomah, a Masai native who was studying in the United States and happened to be in New York on 9/11, spearheaded the idea. He finally made it back to Kenya to visit six months later, where he proposed his idea to his elders. "I didn't want to do it just by donating a cow," he said. "I wanted to involve the elders that raised me, to bless it and make it sacred, to console and comfort a nation that had taken care of me and given me an education, given me a place to live. I just couldn't ignore their pain."

Naiyomah and his tribal elders were under no illusion that fourteen cattle would make any practical difference to a nation with a gross domestic product of $14.2 trillion and 97 million cattle of its own. What makes the gift amazing is how much of themselves they *gave* anyway, with no expectation of receiving anything in return. These Masai touched the hearts of so many people because their deed was such an ultimate expression of solidarity, love, and selfless giving.

"What's in It for Me?"

We live in a world where the predominant question is "What's in it for me?" People associate success, happiness, and love with *getting* things in order to reach those states. By extension, we live in a world where most people perceive that they are *lacking*, and people expend tremendous amounts of energy and time trying to get what they believe they lack.

For example, people believe they lack money—no matter how much they get, they believe they lack more—so extreme amounts of energy are spent on pursuing more. Studies show, however, that once people make enough for the basic necessities, like shelter and food, there is no correlation between money and happiness. When people pursue money in the belief that they are pursuing happiness, it can actually be quite harmful. According to the Princeton researcher Daniel Kahneman, who shared the 2002 Nobel Prize for applying the principles of psychology to economics, "This focusing illusion may lead to a misallocation of time, from accepting lengthy commutes (which are among the worst moments of the day) to sacrificing time spent socializing (which are among the best moments of the day). The long-term effect of income gains becomes relatively small because attention shifts to less novel aspects of daily life."

As another example, in the typical conception of a relationship today, the focus is on how good the other person is going to make someone feel about himself or herself—"What's in it for me, what will I get?"—versus a commitment to give attention, understanding, compromise, and other forms of loving action to enable each other and the relationship itself to prosper. In today's narcissistic mode, so many people can't even seem to comprehend the idea of giving of themselves and working together on areas of challenge to make a relationship work. Instead, they are fiercely dedicated to analyzing how good the other person is at making them feel better about themselves. Search for what is lacking, and things will always be found; as such, people dispose of relationships as if these were cell phones that no longer met their needs, and off they go shopping for that next someone who they hope will be a more perfect "yes" man or woman.

A society addicted to getting is a society based on a belief of lack: never rich enough, time enough, stuff enough, pretty enough, thin enough, big enough, loved enough, appreciated enough, or good enough. A society based on a belief of lack is one where its people will be frustrated, anxious, depressed, and angry and will feel overwhelmed and insignificant, no matter how much they make and acquire. People in a society like that may survive for longer years, and they may live amid lots of cool-looking stuff, but they will merely survive at the expense of thriving.

Fortunately, there is a growing awareness that living a life that is rich in kindness and giving is the key to living a rich life. Academic research in this area has been surging, and the work of the University of California researcher Sonja Lyubomirsky and her colleagues is among the most cited in this area. Her most renowned findings are that while genetics account for about 50 percent of happiness, and life circumstances such as geographic location and marital status account for another 10 percent, the remaining 40 percent of happiness is determined by "intentional activity"—the experiences you choose to devote your energy to. In another of her studies, participants had to perform five simple acts of nonmonetary kindness per week for six weeks, such as helping a friend write a paper or visiting the elderly. While participants in the control group who did no kind acts showed no gains in happiness, those who performed acts of giving showed significant increases in happiness during the period. A recent Harvard study, meanwhile, suggests a strong link between giving financial gifts such as charitable donations and increased happiness, while another demonstrates that spending money on others makes people far happier than spending it on themselves (in fact, spending money on oneself showed no correlation to increased happiness).

Thank You for Reading This

Giving to others, instead of seeking to get, is a close sibling to giving thanks, also known as gratitude, whose opposite is the perception of lack. In recent years, a lot of research has also demonstrated a strong link between gratitude and happiness. For example, several recent studies conducted by Todd Kashdan, an associate professor of psychology at George Mason University, showed that gratitude is one of the most important ingredients for living a good life. (Interestingly, Kashdan found that men feel and express far less gratitude than women do.)

Further suggesting a growing awareness of the power of giving and gratitude, mainstream books on the topic have also surged in recent years. The television broadcaster and journalist Deborah Norville's *Thank You Power* translates a lot of the academic research into an engaging and useful read. In a *Newsweek* interview about the book, Norville said she was driven to write it because "I noticed that when I focused on what was going well in my life—as opposed to fixating on the problems that crept up—I was happier and things worked out better for me."

The key word in Norville's response is "focused," because reading about the benefits of giving and gratitude here likely makes sense to you in theory. The point, though, is to actively focus on the different areas of your life to see how much giving to others and how much giving thanks you are really *doing*—rather than fixating on what you don't have and want to get—in order to consciously increase them.

It can be quite challenging to honestly and clearly assess how much you seek to get, versus how much you seek to give, and how grateful you are for what you've got, versus how much you lament what you perceive you lack, in the various areas of your life—especially relationships. The ego can be a stubborn donkey that wants you to believe that yes, greed and selfishness are really big problems, but they are problems *other people* have. To protect its own selfishness, for example, the ego tends to focus on those one or two times you were kind and giving, while shielding your consciousness from the thirty-five times you reacted from emotions because you weren't getting what you want. If necessary, visualize stepping away from your own body and ego and assessing from your wise, higher consciousness how much you focus on getting and on lack in your relationships, finances, career, and more. No matter how selfish you acknowledge you are, forgive yourself immediately, and realize that you have just made great gains by discovering so many untapped opportunities to give, be kind, and be grateful.

If you escalate how much you give and how grateful you are, life shines brighter instantly. When you experience how generosity and gratitude relieve you of stress and the feeling of being in a never-ending fight—how they instead tickle your mind and spirit and help you manifest greater joy, clarity, and purpose throughout your life—you then naturally come to view situations and people in terms of how you can give to them and what you are grateful for within them, versus what you can take from them, what they lack, and how they threaten you. The experiential equivalent of giving away fourteen head of cattle that are very sacred to you or giving away a sizable chunk of the money or the time that is so valuable to you becomes more than second nature; it becomes as necessary an experience as sleeping or eating.

No matter how much you believe you are already committed to kindness, giving, being grateful, and doing unto others as you would have them do unto you, do the following exercises. Or even if you still doubt that investing your energy in giving more than in getting, as fluffy and nice as it may sound, is really worth it, do the following exercises. I give you my word, my sacred cattle, that the revelations you experience by doing these Give to *Really* Live exercises will speak for themselves.

Five Intense Questions for You
1. What are five of the kindest and most selfless things people ever did for you?
2. What are three of the kindest and most selfless things you ever did for others, where you genuinely expected nothing in return?
3. In what areas of your life do you tend to perceive the most lack? Relationships? Finances? Can you envision how shifting away from what you want to get to what you will give enables you to take responsibility, set the example, and shift this perception?
4. What is the most valuable thing you have that you would be willing to give up if you knew with certainty that it would save a stranger's life?
5. If you won $10 million, how much would you donate to charity? Which charities and why? What proportion of your income are you willing to (or do you already) donate today to these charities?

Give to *Really* Live Exercises

Exercise 1: Create Wish Lists of a Different Sort

When my sister and I were children, my mother always handed us the thick-as-a-brick Sears catalog several weeks before Christmas and let us list the toys we most wanted from it. She would then forward our toy wishes to Santa. Come Christmas, I actually received several of the dozens of toys I had chosen. By association, I really came to love the ink-and-paper smell of catalogs and still do today!

Perhaps you also created wish lists of what you wanted for the holidays when you were young. Maybe you have since kept on creating such lists, formally in writing or by the thoughts you think: what you want in a mate, in a home, in a job, and so on. These lists all tend to share one thing in common: they're all about what you want to *get*. Yet although that can be fun the way it was when you were young, I also caution you that it can be quite self-sabotaging, because you are an adult, and you, not your parents or even Santa, are responsible for yourself.

When was the last time, if ever, that you created a list of what you intended to *give* to a particular situation? It is a strong demonstration of just how much of a "What's in it for me?" society we're in, of how deeply its tendrils have sunk in, that the idea of giving lists may seem so strange, initially. Shouldn't you be putting what you *want* out there, in order to attract it into your life? Isn't that how it works? The popular and diluted impression of the Law of Attraction notwithstanding, no.

First of all, the longer you've lived and the more you have paid attention to your life, the more you have likely realized that things happen for a reason, even if you don't understand the reasons at the time, and that often what you wanted so badly is not the thing you really needed. Consider past significant others in your life, for a convenient example; you may have prayed to keep them, been convinced they were right for you, and been certain that your world would collapse without them. Now, in retrospect, you may realize that this was anything but true, and you may even laugh about how badly you wanted them.

Second, if you keep announcing what you want to get, this is a repeated announcement that you lack something, that you are less than complete, that there is emptiness inside you that something external must fill. This state ironically and most definitely contributes to the rust and the crust inside you that blocks you from being who you know you really are. There is nothing wrong with desiring anything, such as a great job, a nice home, or a steady relationship. But remember that you are an active adult player in achieving whatever it is you desire, not a passive and helpless baby who must depend on others for what you want. The *only* part you have any say in and control over, in fact, is what you will *give*, what you will do, to make it happen. So, what are you willing to give, what do you wish to give, to achieve what you value?

For whatever big goals you have in life, therefore, make wish-to-give lists. What do you intend to give that man or woman who is or will be your lifelong partner? Will you give patience, tolerance, your commitment to communication, space, and plenty of hugs and kisses? What do you intend to give of yourself in your dream job? What do you intend to give in order to repair your relationship with an estranged loved one or friend? What do you intend to give in order to lose or gain weight?

Write down how you intend to give of yourself—what is in your power to *do* that you will therefore commit to doing—and review it periodically. This is a highly effective way to stay on your path to your goals and greater truth. By putting it "out there for the world," getting it out of your mind and onto paper, you will attract that which values what you value and intend to give.

"I want a relationship where I can really trust the man."

"I will give 110 percent dedication to making sure the man I am in a relationship with can trust me."

Notice the profound difference between these two statements? Which is really more likely to attract the right man?

Exercise 2: Do Kind Things and Make Sure No One Knows It

During the next week or so, commit at least five acts of kindness, and be certain that no one ever knows it. Yes, people like to get recognition for the kind things they do, but the deepest acts of giving are those in which nothing—not even awareness and acknowledgment by the recipient or anyone else—is expected or desired in return.

Have some fun planning your surreptitious kindness plan of attack. Will you include several people you know and some strangers, too? What kind acts can you think of where you, the unknown giver, won't be detected, and how will you do them?

Consider weeding your neighbor's flower garden or shoveling snow off her driveway when she is out. Or maybe putting five $10 bills in separate envelopes, writing "Have a Nice Day" on each envelope, and then sticking the envelopes in people's mailboxes or under the windshield wipers of their cars. Before anyone gets to your workplace in the morning, you could place a full-size candy bar on every person's desk. Those are a few suggestions to get your own ideas flowing. Are these examples of acts I've actually done myself? Well, reread the rules of this exercise if you have to ask!

Exercise 3: Send Three Letters of Gratitude

During the next week or two, write at least three letters of gratitude to different people in your life, and give the letters to each of them. Researchers at Kent State University have found that taking the time to write letters of appreciation to others is a particularly powerful way to let gratitude make you happier. Type the letters, or write them by hand to ensure even deeper contemplation and personalization. If you cannot hand-deliver them, mail the letters via the post office, versus e-mail; people are used to quick-reading e-mails, but, because of things like the tactile feel of the paper and the increasing rarity of meaningful mail via postal service, they'll give deeper attention to a paper letter and cherish it much more.

The possibilities for whom to target these letters to are as vast as the number of people who have played any sort of role in your life. Former teachers or bosses or your childhood friends? With at least one of your letters, consider targeting someone who, on reflection, you may be taking for granted. For example and as covered in the Dive Deeper into Your Blood experience, it is easy to fall into surface-y patterns with the "everyday people," such as your spouse, children, parents, or work mates, but these very people would benefit greatly from hearing what you are grateful for and most appreciate about them.

With another of your letters, I urge you to target someone with whom you currently have a shaky or downright volatile relationship or someone who is simply difficult to deal with. Everyone has some positive attributes, something to admire and learn from, although it can take a fair amount of clearing our own hearts and eyes to see it. By taking the time to discover the positive attributes of, and contributions from, whomever you choose, and then describing these in a kind letter, you achieve several worthwhile goals. First, many people who seem argumentative, crabby, mean, or otherwise difficult to deal with are often transformed in ways small and large by such acts of kindness. Such people are often caught in a vicious cycle: they may have faced so much confrontation and resistance earlier in their lives that they trained themselves to expect it, which in turn makes them seem confrontational and resistant to others, which in turn provokes more of it back to them, and so on. A kind letter expressing thanks and praise throws a wrench in that vicious cycle, sometimes more than you can imagine. Second, writing such a letter is another great way to teach yourself to look for the good in all people and situations, versus focusing on the negative and the lack. This shift in perspective alone will turn your life toward greater happiness.

Exercise 4: Read Real Good

Try to read at least one of the following books and see as many movies from the following list as possible during the week or two that you concentrate on doing the other exercises in this Intense Experience.

Books

A Christmas Carol, Charles Dickens. You know the story. But reading this, the ultimate novel about the power of kindness and compassion, while engaged in these other Give to *Really* Live exercises, is an especially transformative experience.

The Force of Kindness: Change Your Life with Love and Compassion, Sharon Salzberg. Through stories and meditations in this book-and-CD combination, the Buddhist teacher Sharon Salzberg gently shows readers what kindness means and provides simple steps to help you experience the power of giving and kindness immediately.

Thanks: How the New Science of Gratitude Can Make You Happier, Robert Emmons. This wonderful book by the University of California–Davis professor Robert Emmons, one of today's foremost authorities on gratitude, follows his own groundbreaking studies that demonstrate how giving and gratitude can dramatically improve the lives of people who are committed to them.

Thank You Power: Making the Science of Gratitude Work for You, Deborah Norville. The broadcast journalist Deborah Norville has written one of the most inspiring, well-researched, entertaining, and immediately useful books among the many released in recent years on how to improve your relationships, career, health, and other aspects of life with the power of gratitude.

Why Good Things Happen to Good People: The Exciting New Research That Proves the Link between Doing Good and Living a Longer, Healthier, Happier Life, Steven Post and Jill Neimark. Stephen Post, a leading academic authority on altruism, presents deep evidence that a life committed to giving to others and doing good is key to living longer, avoiding depression and stress, increasing feelings of happiness, and achieving one's goals, including financial ones. The book is filled with things you can do, starting now, to realize these benefits and includes a very revealing self-test as well.

Movies

Answering the Call: Ground Zero's Volunteers

Art of Peace: His Holiness the Dalai Lama

Children of Heaven

The Life a House Built: The 25th Anniversary of the Jimmy & Rosalynn Carter Work Project

The Lives of Others

Marianne Williamson—Everyday Grace

Mother Teresa (narrated by Richard Attenborough)

Patch Adams

Pay It Forward

Schindler's List

Simon Birch

Sister Helen

Sugihara—Conspiracy of Kindness

A Tale of Two Cities

The Ultimate Gift

A Walk to Remember

Exercise 5: What Causes Ignite You?

"Never doubt that a small group of thoughtful, committed citizens can change the world; indeed, it's the only thing that ever has," said cultural anthropologist Margaret Mead.

Where do you believe change is most needed? When you read the news, when you're in conversation, and when you're just thinking alone, what causes really stir your heart and spark your passions? And to what extent are you giving your time and energy to those causes?

A response like, "I'd love to volunteer, but I'm just so busy" is still common at this point. We've been discussing this favorite American refrain—"I'm just so busy!"—since the Journey Back to Neverland experience. If you've read this far and gone through exercises within the experiences, your perception of where you are dedicating your time and energy, and of how much time and energy you really have, has likely shifted. If you haven't gone through actually *doing* (versus reading about) many of the exercises in this book yet, please do yourself an immense favor and do them, if you'd like to stop feeling as if you don't have enough time or energy. You have been given exactly the amount of time and energy you need in this world. How you spend it to achieve greater energy, clarity, inner peace, and happiness—or misspend it to run yourself into ruts and keep yourself there—is the question. One of the most powerful methods of attaining that energy, clarity, inner peace, and happiness is to dedicate your time and energy is to volunteer for your favorite causes.

Have fun deciding which causes really inspire you that you would like to volunteer for, and then do it. Animal shelters, food pantries, mentoring programs, museums, theaters, homeless shelters, or environmental programs? Perhaps you have special skills that certain nonprofit organizations really need, such as health-care licensing or carpentry. There is never a shortage of opportunities for volunteer work; www.VolunteerMatch.org is a great place to discover some opportunities that would be ideal for you.

Charities and nonprofits definitely need financial donations, too, and I'd encourage you to also give to your preferred cause. Determine how much you can donate on a routine basis, and then give at least a little bit more than that.

It is true that you work to make your money, so in essence you are volunteering your time to the charities you donate money to; however, if you have never actually donated your time *directly* to any cause, I would encourage you to do so in the next week or two (along with donating money), to personally experience the soul-clearing benefits. Finally, if you are concerned about how the money you donate is spent by a given charity, head to www .charitywatch.org, which monitors and grades the charities.

Exercise 6: The Ocean of Gratitude List

If I were to write a self-hurt book called *How to Be Miserable*, it would be one sentence long: "Spend as much energy as possible focusing on what you don't have." Of course, this is advice that so many people already seem to be taking, so I am writing this instead.

As long as you are alive, you have an infinite ocean of things in your life for which to be grateful. It could literally take the rest of your life and then some for you to create a complete list of things that you are grateful for! And that's something to be grateful for.

You don't need to spend your entire life creating that complete list, but you can start by making a list of forty things that you are grateful for. Then each day, add at least one item to your ever-growing, drop-in-the-ocean gratitude list.

Why start by creating a list of at least forty things that you are grateful for? Because, like warming up the engine of a boat that hasn't been used for some time, it will get your mind, heart, and spirit revved up in the gratitude mode. Then post your list of forty items where you will be able to see it, and pen in at least one new thing you are grateful for daily.

To get you started, here are just some random items off of my own drop-in-the-ocean gratitude list: Cheese. Summer in Chicago. My son's good health. Air conditioning. The band Arcade Fire. My MacBook Pro. Free tennis courts. Cormac McCarthy. My sister. Thunderstorms. Heated car seats. Contact lenses. My hands, especially the opposing thumbs. Spinach.

Start your list as soon as possible, and keep it going to maintain a healthy perspective. And if you are grateful for anything on my little list, feel free to copy.

Exercise 7: Regain Awareness of All That You Have, Then Give It All Away

Day in and day out, people move through their own lives with little to no awareness of all that they've got. This is true of the intangible things, beyond material objects, the gifts of greatest substance that people lose sight of. Yet often to our great surprise, it can especially be seen and readily experienced if we become reawakened to all of the material possessions we have.

If you are at home now, or the next time you are, put on some new eyes. Instead of moving through your rooms and all of your stuff following your usual patterns, in which you are conscious only of what you might immediately need, wander through your home as if you were an alien. Notice all of the stuff. Open cabinets. Gaze into closets. See and touch and recognize the amazing amount of stuff. Utensils, photos, electronics, pillows, paper clips, jewelry, cleaning supplies, shoes, pots, paper goods, plants, furniture, and the list can go on and on. You likely have a lot of stuff. The older you are, the more stuff you probably have.

Looking at it through those fresh eyes, ask yourself, What in the world is all this stuff? How can one person have so much stuff? Once you have become aware of the great volume of stuff you are so fortunate to have, shift to a deeper level of consciousness in yourself. Pick any item in your home—a cup, a picture, a plant, a pillow—and recall how that thing came into your life. When did you buy it or receive it as a gift? Who were you with? What were you thinking and feeling at the time you got or received it? There is a story behind each and every object in your home; some of the stories are not exactly fascinating, but others are. And every item, even those that seem mundane, carries some type of mood related to its story. Wander through your home recognizing the objects and recalling their stories and the subtle moods they each evoke.

In doing so, it is first of all impossible not to feel gratitude for all that you've got and the richness of life and experience represented in each of those things. Yet this is also an exercise to determine whether there are any things in your home that you have not been consciously recognizing but that may be subtly evoking certain moods in you on a subconscious level. For example, is there a shirt in your closet you may have bought during a particularly stressful time in your life, such as during a breakup or after losing a job, and could that shirt still be subtly evoking feelings of stress in you? When you consciously assess the stuff in your home—and your car and office—you will discover that many of the objects carry messages beyond their function, and you may not want some of those messages around.

As the final and biggest step in this powerful exercise, give stuff away. You will likely realize that you have an abundance, if not an overabundance, of things. Gather stuff up—certainly, the items whose messages you don't want around and possessions that you simply don't use, but also some of the things that *do* have value and meaning to you—and give them away. Give away things you don't want, which is easy, but also give away some of the things you would really like to keep.

Invite your family and friends over, especially those who may be in a tight spot financially, and host a ceremonial party offering them some of these things. Tag all of the items throughout your home that you will be giving away. Serve food and refreshments, have some really upbeat music playing, and let them wander and take whatever they want to take that you have tagged. If two people want the same thing, set up some fun games to determine who will get it.

Of course, there are charities that also need these things you no longer want and objects you do want but are graciously giving away. If you are especially adventurous and would like to witness surprise, confusion, and joy on strangers' faces, take several things of great value that you are willing to give away; head off to a place where people may be in need, such as certain neighborhoods or shelters; and offer your things to the people you encounter there. If anyone is hesitant to take your valuable stuff, simply explain that you are giving it away because you have more than you will ever need, you lack for nothing, and you wanted someone to have it who may need it more than you do.

Exercise 8: Get Crazy with Kindness

Shake yourself up, uncork yourself, and spray the kindness inside you all around like Champagne. For the next week or two, make it a conscious point to dramatically escalate the kind words and acts you give to others. When you do, be aware of how extensively your perspective on your life and the mood changes; hopefully, you've been recording your thoughts and feelings with all of the exercises in a journal or the like, but give extra attention in your journal to your internal feedback from this exercise.

To get crazy with the kindness, make it a point to compliment something about absolutely everyone you encounter. From your children to the man behind the deli counter, train yourself to look for something to praise, and do so—their vibrant eyes, the confident way they walk, their ties or earrings, or their contagious laugh, for example. Watch how a simple compliment alone completely shifts people's disposition!

Be especially vigilant in complimenting people with whom you may typically have a rough or disturbingly silent relationship, such as certain difficult people at work. If you have any doubt about the unbelievably transformative power of giving and kindness, pay attention to what happens when you give your "opponent" or "enemy" an honest compliment. A little compliment about his watch or her shoes is good. A larger compliment (as long as it is sincere!) about some character aspect, such as her work ethic or his eloquent communication skills, is even better. Paying a compliment and then asking him or her for guidance is the best, such as, "You know, I've always appreciated how clearly you communicate in memos. The next time I write a memo, would you mind taking a quick look to let me know how to make it more concise?" This is the deepest form of compliment, because you are saying that you appreciate the person so much that you want to learn from him or her. Watch and you'll see positive cataclysmic shifts that this kindness creates in your currently difficult relationships!

In addition to compliments, be on the lookout for every opportunity to help people around you. Open doors for people, give up your seat on the bus, help a mother with kids by carrying her bags, wash the dishes even if it is some other family member's responsibility, and help your neighbor around the yard. Give unexpected gifts to people as well—especially people you don't normally give gifts to. Research has shown that giving people experiences versus giving them material goods tends to make them much happier, so consider surprising people with movie theater tickets or restaurant gift certificates or this wonderful book I know of called *The 9 Intense Experiences*.

Make it a point to really give people your undivided attention as well. Listening to another person, versus wanting to be heard, is an endangered species, so in your conversations with people, commit to really hearing what they are saying. And try hard not to cut off anyone who is in a conversation with you; give the person the respect of letting him or her speak and be fully heard.

Finally, give out plenty of hugs. Even if you are Incredibly Macho and believe hugs are for girls and their puppies and that the right way to greet or say good-bye to someone is to butt heads, note that research has found that the simple act of hugging another person releases the hormone oxytocin, which protects against heart disease (note, too, that no such research exists for butting heads). Oxytocin, known as the "love hormone," also plays a big role in strengthening all sorts of social bonds, from sexual and romantic to friendships and even establishing trust among strangers. Hugs are good for everyone involved in them! It is another telling sign of our society that so many people are still embarrassed to give or receive hugs; be the change you want to see in the world. Hug lots, and hug well.

If you think it may be a challenge for you to remember to commit kind acts—if you're in the grocery store and your natural inclination is to rush to the shortest checkout line before another person gets there, versus letting him or her pass in front of you—I suggest that you use memory devices to keep you on the kindness track. I have written a big red X on the back of my hand in the past to remind myself to commit kind acts throughout the day. Life-coaching clients of mine have written "Be Nice!" or similar words on Post-It notes and stuck them up on doors, on car dash-boards, on mirrors, above their computers, and in other places where they're sure to see them throughout the day. Do whatever it takes to go kindness crazy for a week or two. Pay attention to how you feel during this time (you're going to love it). Don't be surprised at all when after the week or two are up, your craziness just naturally persists.

Intense Experience #8

✺

Embrace Death and
Dance the Night Away

Live as if you were to die tomorrow, learn as if you were to live
forever.

—*Gandhi*

The last suit that you wear, you don't need any pockets.

—*Wayne Dyer*

Perhaps the whole root of our trouble, the human trouble, is that
we will sacrifice all the beauty of our lives, will imprison ourselves
in totems, taboos, crosses, blood sacrifices, steeples, mosques,
races, armies, flags, nations, in order to deny the fact of death,
which is the only fact we have.

—*James Baldwin*

Death helps us to see what is worth trusting and loving and what
is a waste of time.

—*J. Neville Ward*

I've cited various statistics throughout this book, but
here are the two I find most alarming: 100 percent of all
Americans who are no longer alive are now dead. And 100 percent

of all Americans who are still living will someday die. I'm told the statistics are at or near the same levels in other countries throughout the world, with the possible exception of Denmark.

It seems that death is our most chronic condition of all, but that's not what is of concern. As sure as the trees will fall and become the soil, that's just the beautiful and inevitable reality. The problem is that people are in great denial of the fact of their own death. They expend so much time, money, and energy trying to run and hide from it that they forget to live. Yet by embracing death respectfully, like a lover we know in our heart we will someday meet again, and dancing the night away, we can fully realize our lives.

To say that our culture is youth-obsessed is a vast understatement. Although the median age in the United States is thirty-seven, people accept it as perfectly normal that the faces that dominate advertisements, movies, and magazines are a good ten to twenty years younger. By far, the most popular forms of entertainment are youth-dominated, such as music (*American Idol*'s cutoff point for participants is age twenty-eight) and sports (in the four most-watched American sports—football, baseball, basketball, and hockey—age forty is considered elderly). It is no coincidence that Stephenie Meyer's *Twilight* series of books—featuring beautiful, young, immortal vampires—is the cultural phenomenon of our time, with the books already selling more than 85 million copies worldwide and the film adaptations grossing nearly $1 billion thus far.

Meanwhile, Americans had more than 10 million cosmetic surgeries and body-modification procedures in 2008, with Botox treatments and breast augmentation being the two most popular. Even with the Great Recession prompting the first *dip* in 2008 in this category overall after ten years of explosive growth, pectoral implants, cheek implants, and buttock lifts only increased in popularity. And more than $20 billion is spent on cosmetics and beauty aids in the United States annually; the products that dominate are, not surprisingly, those most heavily advertised in print and on TV, and when you recall those ads, what types of faces come to mind? There is nothing wrong with trying to look attractive or even with looking like you're trying too hard to look attractive. But lurking within these numbers—numbers that have grown astronomically over the decades—is the fact that people are increasingly trying to distort the outward reality of the two things that everyone most certainly is: (1) imperfect, and (2) getting older and closer to death.

Wait, This Is Not Bad News!

Don't run from this chapter as if I'm the bearer of depressing news. I realize that honestly discussing death is our society's great taboo, far more so than discussing sex or even money. If you feel the least bit uncomfortable with this topic right now, that is precisely the point. Your spirit may be perfect, but your mind and body are anything but. They're both made of shifting stuff, and although that stuff can be prolonged in form through healthy living and maybe also a few scientific tricks such as cryogenics and philosopher's stones, as sure as all plants, animals, and stars themselves die and have their energy and matter transformed into something else, you will someday die. Me, too. That's not bad news. That's not depressing. That's something certain, and it's a precious gift.

Yes, it is sad and frightening that you and I will someday be dead, and that whether it comes fast or slow, we will have to go through the process of dying, which is a separate and, for many, even greater fear. These fears are as old as humanity itself, and I have still not heard of any culture where, through mind-set and ritual, these fears were routinely overcome. Yet it is not about overcoming the fears. It is about accepting them and embracing the reality of death and dying, in order to fully embrace the gift of this precious life, versus hiding from it, tucking it away, trivializing it, and in effect denying it and squandering this priceless and limited life.

In other cultures, past and present, the dead and the dying have been on full display for families and communities. In his book *The History of Death: Burial Customs and Funeral Rites, from the Ancient World to Modern Times*, the author Michael Kerrigan profiles how throughout human history all over the world, dying has been a very open affair routinely witnessed by family, friends, and strangers. Funerals and death rites, too, have largely been open affairs that are normally and oftentimes ceremoniously witnessed by community members who didn't even know the deceased. With death and dying more common sights (and smells) in those communities than McDonald's is in ours, the reality of one's own death—maybe decades hence, maybe tomorrow—had to be faced. The fears had to be confronted and embraced, both within one's own heart and within the community. Kerrigan noted how many Slavic communities embraced death and the fear of it together: "Mock funerals (sometimes with real bodies) were a centerpiece of the Christmas frivolities." On the island of Sumba in Indonesia, "It has come to be accepted that an important funeral is too big an occasion to be missed—even by the individual whose funeral it is." Those who can afford to do so attend a funeral in their honor while they are still alive (often even tourists to Sumba are encouraged to attend).

Everyone Lives Forever in America

Contrast that with death and dying in the United States. Americans do not drive, walk, bike, or jog around and routinely witness death. On the rare occasion that they do, such as in an obviously fatal car accident, it is an extremely disturbing situation that people want to erase from their minds. Americans do not routinely visit homes where people are dying. Dying is rarely done in the home at all; it is quietly tucked away in hospitals, hospices, and long-term care centers, where only the closest family and friends visit. While Latin Americans have their Day of the Dead on November 1, in which they collectively visit graves to bestow gifts on the departed, Americans have no equivalent public celebration on which they pay respects to the dead and visit graves. The intention of Memorial Day was to honor soldiers who have died in service to the United States, but it is now a day for picnics and the "Sale of the Season!" Although Halloween has roots in a Celtic festival called Samhain, during which people believed they could communicate with and placate the dead, today it is an occasion to dress up like ghouls or superheroes and get lots of candy or drink lots of beer. As for wakes and funerals, only people who knew the deceased would even think to attend one in the United States. They're closed and somber affairs, unlike the big parties celebrating dead people's lives in many cultures, such as in parts of Madagascar and Ireland. Although cremation is less expensive and perhaps better for the environment than burial is, the fact that nearly 40 percent of all bodies in the United States are now cremated, and this number is projected to rise to nearly 60 percent by 2025, strongly suggests that people cannot stomach the idea of flesh decomposing, because that indicates mortality. You may want to run away even after reading that right now.

Yes, Americans and other Westerners fear death and dying as everyone else does, but instead of facing and embracing it, we've collectively become masters at denying it. The American Psychiatric Association noted more than a decade ago that by the time American kids reach eighteen, they will have seen 16,000 simulated murders and 200,000 acts of violence. With the phenomenal increase in video game play in the last decade alone, that number has certainly risen. Aside from the degree to which all of this violence leads to more violent people, this is trivialization of death to the umpteenth degree. In how many of those 16,000 murders are the victims' dying and death, including their personal stories, their funerals, and their families' grieving process, even a minor focal point? In virtually all cases, they are the mere equivalent of stick figures, present for a moment on the screen and then simply obliterated. Out of sight, out of mind, then on to the next action sequence or commercial. There is no confronting and embracing the fact of death, no hovering about the corpses and pondering our own mortality, simply pure denial of it.

As David Wendell Moller, a faculty member of the Program in Medical Ethics at the Indiana University School of Medicine and a sociology professor at the School of Liberal Arts, wrote in his book *Life's End: Technocratic Dying in an Age of Spiritual Yearning*: "In the modern context in which dying has lost its meaningfulness, death is viewed as failure. This fact helps explain the great sense of shame and humiliation that dying persons and their loved ones feel. In addition, many physicians view death as defeat and failure on both a personal and professional level. As long as dying is seen as shameful and death is viewed as failure, open and honest communication will be stymied. Simply, no one likes to talk about their shortcomings or failures. These, instead, are remanded to the isolated, invisible realm of our collective human experience. That is to say, they are, in fact, denied."

So, Do the Tango Already

Yet as those who have tended to the dying know, death and dying are not shameful, bad, wrong, or humiliating. As Moller went on to suggest, and I agree, death may be making a comeback. That is to say, the social—and self-destructive—denial of death may be waning, slowly, in the Western world. Perhaps beginning with Elisabeth Kubler-Ross's seminal book *On Death and Dying* in 1969 and as evidenced in various popular plays, self-help books, novels, and films since then, there is a growing countercultural contingent who are embracing the fact of their death and dancing the night away. People's planning their own funerals is starting to grow in popularity, and, as covered in a *New York Times* article on July 20, 2006, titled, "It's My Funeral and I'll Serve Ice Cream If I Want To," the baby boom generation is leading the self-planning charge with some very nontraditional and more celebration-oriented, rather than somber, funerals (including Harry Ewell, who, as he planned when alive, had mourners at his 2003 burial treated to ice cream from the ice cream truck he used to drive).

I invite you, with all due respect, to join the party. By running, hiding, fighting, and denying death, people ironically devote so much of their energy to it; death will take your energy and do what it wants with it when your time comes anyway, so why give so much of your life away to it before then? Struggling against anything consumes an awful lot of energy. Embrace the undeniable reliability of it instead, and dance gracefully, let it teach you, and, as with all loving embraces, let it increase your energy and desire to live now. Use that energy and knowledge to really live your one sure life in those mortal flesh and bones.

Five Intense Questions for You
1. Some people are afraid that by thinking about their own deaths, they're somehow going to bring about death sooner. Others are afraid that by walking underneath a ladder, they will die within seven years. What irrational fears and superstitions do you hold about death, and where might they have stemmed from?
2. Who are the closest people in your life who have died? What are the greatest lessons, if any, you learned from their deaths?
3. Are you afraid of dying? Are you afraid of death? Why?
4. To what extent are you in denial of your own death? If you believe you are not in denial, do you make a point of living every day fully and completely, as if it could be your last?
5. What do you hope happens to people when they die?

Embrace Death and Dance the Night Away Exercises

Exercise 1: Go to a Cemetery and Raise the Dead

Breathe easy, you won't need a pickax or a shovel. For this exercise, all you need to do is take walks through cemeteries and raise the departed you encounter there through contemplation. In earlier eras in the United States, cemeteries were a much more integrated part of people's daily experience. Churches with cemeteries on or near their properties were built in the centers of towns, and because daily life was a lot more localized and people moved about much more on foot, they encountered the tombstones of family, friends, neighbors, and strangers—and the awareness that the departed were entombed six feet below—with great regularity. The reminder of people who were once here and who had also loved, laughed, struggled, hoped, and dreamed and were now gone, the reminder of one's own mortality, was always near.

Take slow walks in cemeteries, especially the charming old ones dating back hundreds of years or longer. You may already routinely visit the gravesite of someone you have loved and lost, and that can certainly be a very powerful and necessary experience, but in this case, visit graveyards of those you never personally knew. Feel the serenity of the place as you walk along; even old cemeteries in the hearts of cities seem to be shrouded in silence. Read the names on the tombstones. Say them aloud. Read the epitaphs to get a sense of the departed's stories and what they and their loved ones valued. Read the years of birth and death, and pay special attention to the dash or the space in between these dates that represents an entire life.

When you are called to do so by a particular tombstone, stop before it and contemplate. Entombed beneath your feet are the remains of someone who once lived as you are alive now. Who was this person? What might have been her story? How many times did she fall in love? How many times was her heart broken? What kind of work did she do? What kind of mother was she? What did she yearn for? What did she fear? What made her cry? What made her laugh? What did she think about her life as her life came to a close?

You may well receive visions, feelings, and other forms of answers to the questions you ponder about your chosen departed. While standing there, you cannot know for sure whether this is entirely your imagination or something more. (It is very interesting, though, to later try to dig up information on the dead person through town and online archives to see whether any insights you received about him or her are true.) Yet this is primarily about contemplating a person who was once here and is now gone and then looking up and seeing dozens or hundreds or thousands of other such tombstones representing people who were once here and are now gone, too. It is one thing to read or recite how life is short and precious, but it is quite another to let yourself experience through all of the fibers of your being how short and precious it is. How no one and nothing is immortal. And why right now is the time for what matters. These contemplative walks through cemeteries are among the simplest and most powerful means of allowing yourself to often have that necessary experience.

Exercise 2: Enjoy Your Last Supper

The only foods specifically cited in the Bible as being served at Jesus' last supper were bread and wine. Being that this was a Passover Seder meal observance, many believe the traditional foods for that meal would have been served, including two sorts of bitter herbs, such as endive and watercress, another vegetable dipped in salt water, and roasted lamb shank.

What food and drink would you want your last supper to consist of? Plan your meal, prepare it, and then eat it now in honor of that distant day. But please note that this is far more than an exercise in enjoying your favorite foods. Just as Jesus' last supper was meant to be a very tangible and sensual way for his apostles to remember his life story and purpose, preparing and eating what you would choose for your last supper is a tangible, sensual, and therefore powerful way for you to remember and honor the gift, the story, and the purpose of your life right now. You likely already celebrate your birthday with a cake and other symbols of coming into this human world; this is a symbolic acknowledgment that someday you will also depart this human world, and that you therefore intend to live fully and completely here in this space between arrival and departure.

Give this very special celebration the respect it deserves by carefully planning the dinner. Appetizers, soup, main courses, side dishes, desserts? What will the setting for your meal be? Candlelight, fine china and silverware, and crystal glasses, or paper plates and plastic forks? Will you dine alone or with those you love? If it is with others, you can choose to either let them know the purpose of the meal or simply keep that to yourself as you relish their presence.

Give this very special celebration the respect it deserves by preparing the meal with great joy and care, perhaps also with a close family member or friend. And then, most important, when you do sit down to eat, be fully present for the meal. Eat slowly and with all of your senses engaged in every bite and sip. As you eat, you can consider all of the gifts you have in your life right now, you can reflect on your dreams, and you can recommit to becoming who you know you really are in this life. If you choose, you can engage any invited guests in conversations down this avenue in relation to themselves, such as asking each person, "What are three things you most want to accomplish in life before you die?" and the like. Or you can simply let the conversation go where it may and bask in the joy of it all.

As with your birthday, you may want to make Last Supper Day an annual tradition. You may want to encourage family and friends to each host his or her own, too. On that hopefully very distant day of your death, you may or may not be able to actually repeat this last supper for the last time, but you can certainly reflect back on the honor you paid this space before your death by engaging in this Last Supper exercise now.

Exercise 3: Let the Dead and the Dying Teach You

The dead, the dying, and those who love them can often have the clearest perspectives on how to live life. That's why really good books and movies with that theme tend to be some of the most inspiring and thought-provoking works you'll ever read and see. There have been many worthwhile blockbusters in this genre, such as *On Death and Dying* and *Tuesdays with Morrie*. Following are some lesser-known works that I highly recommend.

Books

The Book of Eulogies, edited by Phyllis Theroux. As the news commentator Cokie Roberts said about this book, "In reading about the parts of a life eulogists choose to remember and recount, we learn a great deal about living a well-lived life." It contains excerpts of eloquent eulogies for and by many of the world's most accomplished individuals, such as a eulogy to Johann Sebastian Bach by William F. Buckley and one for Marilyn Monroe by Diana Trilling. Plus, it contains eulogies by famous writers, thinkers, and other public figures to their parents, departed children, and more, and powerful excerpts on grief and what death means.

Cradled All the While: The Unexpected Gifts of a Mother's Death, Sara Corse. In this well-written and moving memoir, a daughter confronts dying and death, and the need to both gain independence from and bond closer to her mother. Virtually anyone who has or will lose someone he or she loves—meaning everyone—will cherish this book.

The History of Death: Burial Customs and Funeral Rites, from the Ancient World to Modern Times, **Michael Kerrigan.** This is an endlessly fascinating book on how different cultures in the present and the past have experienced and dealt with death, dying, and grieving, from wild celebrations that even allowed incest to the Lakota Sioux practice of leaving new corpses in trees for three days to have the flesh eaten by birds and animals and then burying the skeletons. By understanding other cultures' beliefs and traditions, you inevitably become more aware of, and in a healthy way question, your own.

Returning to Earth, **Jim Harrison.** A little masterpiece about a man who, dying slowly from Lou Gehrig's disease, tells his wife stories he has never shared with anyone. Gorgeous and transformative.

Secrets of the Monarch: What the Dead Can Teach Us about Living a Better Life, **Allison DuBois.** Allison is the inspiration for the hit television show *Medium.* In this book, Allison passes on essential life lessons she's learned through communicating with the dead. Whether you believe in mediums and an afterlife or not, this is an interesting and worthwhile read. If you want to understand life, Allison teaches, you must understand death.

Movies

The Barbarian Invasions. This touching and thought-provoking film, the winner of the Academy Award for Best Foreign Language Film for 2003, explores the bonds and challenges between relatives, friends, and lovers in the face of death and ultimately celebrates life and really living it.

Defending Your Life. In this provocative comedy starring Meryl Streep, an advertising executive who hasn't lived up to his potential in life gets killed by a bus. He enters a place called Judgment City, where through a four-day hearing he must revisit and explain the choices he made in his life.

The Diving Bell and the Butterfly. The book and the movie are both exceptional and tell the true story of the former editor-in-chief of *Elle* magazine Dominique Bauby, who suffered a stroke, went into a coma for twenty days, and then came out almost entirely paralyzed. Bauby "wrote" the book by blinking with his left eye a code that corresponded to the alphabet, while an assistant transcribed the words; the book took about two hundred thousand blinks to create. Bauby died a few days after completing the book.

The Green Mile. In this thought-provoking film based on a Stephen King novel, prisoners on death row have to come to terms with their own impending deaths—including the main character, who is actually innocent.

Hearts and Souls. A wonderful comedy about a yuppie who lets four different childhood friends who have died inhabit his body so that they can work out their unfinished business and their regrets in life.

My Life. An advertising executive who has been living the go-go life has terminal cancer and a limited time to live. His wife is pregnant, and it is not likely that he will make it through the birth. So he records his own discussions on his life and his views for his as-yet-unborn child and learns the real value of life in the process.

Exercise 4: Live Your Own Eulogy

And I'm here today to say a final thank you, Sister Rosa, for being a great woman who used your life to serve, to serve us all. That day that you refused to give up your seat on the bus, you, Sister Rosa, changed the trajectory of my life and the lives of so many other people in the world. I would not be standing here today nor standing where I stand every day had she not chosen to sit down.

—Oprah Winfrey, speaking at Rosa Parks's funeral, October 31, 2005

What would you want said about you at your own funeral? What qualities, deeds, and stories would you want to be remembered for? As with Oprah Winfrey's eulogy to Rosa Parks, eulogies are served not only to honor the dead, but also to inspire and be an example to the living, whether it is millions of people or merely your siblings, children, and grandchildren who hear it.

Writing your own eulogy, as if you were someone outside of yourself who knew you well by the actions you took in this life, is a very powerful exercise to enable you to more fully realize who you really are and what you are meant to do in this life to act on that. In writing your own eulogy, you can more clearly see what you are and are not doing now in your life to live the way you want to be remembered for. You can also see where you might be wandering off the path of who you are and where you are wasting your energy.

You may be aware of all of the love, creativity, and compassion inside you, but to what extent are you putting those into action? Writing your own eulogy from the perspective of someone who watched you closely for many years—but was not inside you personally—is an exceptional road map to help you stay committed to fulfilling your intentions and living your values.

As you will discover in *The Book of Eulogies*, recommended earlier, the best eulogies contain the values that the deceased strived to put into action throughout his or her life. This book also contains specific stories and anecdotes that exemplify the departed person's values. What stories from our own life already portray your loving heart, your tenaciousness, your patience, or whatever values you want to live by? What stories that you intend to make a reality will you incorporate into your eulogy?

When you have written your eulogy, read it aloud. Hearing these words that you would want said about you at your funeral makes their imprint on your heart even stronger. Keep your eulogy somewhere safe so that you can periodically return to it, to make sure you are living your life accordingly.

Exercise 5: Create Your Soundtrack to Being Alive

What are your dozen or more power songs? This is not an all-inclusive list of your favorite songs but instead the songs that, whether through the music or the lyrics or both, are in some way most about you. Songs that really make you come alive. These are the songs that you'd want played at your funeral to most convey your spirit in life.

In a British survey, "My Way," as sung by Frank Sinatra, was the most played song at funerals. It was the song played for my grandfather at his funeral. I was ten years old, it was the first funeral I ever attended, and I recall thinking that it would be a good song to play at my own funeral. It still makes my own power songs list. (A few of my other soundtrack songs include "Speak to Me Gently" by Future of Forestry, "Man of the Hour" by Pearl Jam, "Zorba's Dance" by Mikis Theodorakis, "Ode to Joy" by Beethoven, "Float On" by Modest Mouse, "Love Generation" by Bob Sinclair, and "Beautiful Day" by U2.)

Have fun creating a list of your songs, including the order you want them to play in, and then download them for your iPod or burn them onto a CD. Whenever you need to, such as before an important meeting or when you're feeling stressed out, listen to them. Let them revive you and remind you of who you really are and what matters most to you.

Exercise 6: Plan Your Own Funeral and Host It

> They say such nice things about people at their funerals that it makes me sad to realize that I'm going to miss mine by just a few days.
>
> —*Garrison Keillor*

Alright, in terms of how "strange" several of the exercises in this book are, this one may rank right up there with making a tree your best friend. But here is what is really ridiculous: that you are going to miss the one event in which people think about, honor, and celebrate you the most. What a motivating and educational experience if you could be there! In the end you have no choice, of course; you may attend your actual funeral in living spirit, but the rest of you must be dead, or they're not having it. That said, you can plan and host a mock version of your funeral in your home or anywhere you choose, and, as you can already intuit, it will be one of the strangest, most memorable, and most transformative experiences you ever have.

What type of funeral do you want for yourself? Something traditional, according to your religion? A simple, peaceful, and contemplative event? Something highly symbolic of your personal beliefs and life? A vibrant and perhaps even rowdy celebration? What type of décor, food, drink, and music do you want? What kind of ceremonies will take place and why? What clothing do you want to wear when you are laid out and why? And who will be in attendance? Will the funeral you plan primarily consist of the wake, or will it include a procession and a ceremony at the burial site (which, for your mock funeral, can be a simple procession to your backyard, to the woods, to an actual nearby old graveyard, or to a similar site)?

When you have the vision down for your mock funeral, plan it and host it. Perhaps close friends and family members will help you with the planning and the hosting, and maybe they'll be inspired to host their own at another time as well. This is a very different type of get-together for anyone to be invited to, so consider writing up an explanation of the purpose of your mock funeral and anything you ask of the guest to bring or do, such as stories, eulogies, and so on. Yes, many will find this highly unusual, but because people are caught in such patterns of mediocrity in their own lives, you may be quite surprised at how eager they are to attend this interesting, boundary-pushing event of yours.

As far as being laid out at your mock funeral, you can either choose to actually lie there silently on a table with your eyes closed for a while or have something symbolize you. If you have asked individuals to come to you and pay you last respects privately as you lie there, this can be the most challenging part of the mock funeral. Some people may find it difficult to say what they'd really say privately if you were dead, because you are actually so very alive, and they just aren't internally in the place to be able to do that. Others may not be able to resist saying silly things. You, trying to lie there as still as a corpse, may burst out laughing multiple times. Good! So what? This is not an exercise in funeral perfection. It is an exercise in discovering how people close to you perceive and honor you and how they don't (which may be awareness that sparks a change in you). It is a celebration of your life that you invite others to partake in, whether in a peaceful and contemplative manner or a jubilant one. It's the closest you may get to having an experience like Scrooge in *A Christmas Carol* or George Bailey in *It's a Wonderful Life,* in which you can witness the impact you've had on other people's lives and the impact you *could* have. It's a powerful lesson for living your life and a really fun one at that!

Exercise 7: Get Up and Live!

This is often a difficult but extremely transformative exercise for people; the deeper into the visualization you can go, the more of a shift you tend to experience. In silent solitude and preferably lying down somewhere, such as on your bed, on the couch, or in the sand, close your eyes and visualize that you can no longer move, speak, or communicate in any way with anyone in the outside world. You are still conscious, though, and you know that any day, hour, or minute will be your last before you die and go wherever the dead go. You are lying there on your deathbed. The time is the present—the day you choose to do this exercise and not some day in the future.

- Where does your mind go? To what people, periods, and stories in your life do you go? What happy memories drift back to you that you are most grateful for?

- Whose face comes to mind that causes your heart to ache, because maybe you should have made that commitment, taken that leap, made that phone call, let those barriers go, taken that journey, felt the fear but done it anyway?
- What big goals did you have that were never achieved, because you made yourself believe it wasn't possible now, but that someday soon you would get to it for sure?
- What new experiences did you always mean to try but didn't, because you convinced yourself that you were too busy, too poor, too tired, or too something now, but you'd surely try it someday soon?
- What did you always mean to say that you never said and to whom?
- Whom should you have forgiven and for what, and from whom and for what should you have asked forgiveness?
- What do you regret doing and not having done, as you lie there on your deathbed in the present time, unable to communicate with anyone else?

Watch out for your ego, which will try to run interference when particularly painful truths begin to surface: for example, "I might have missed him dearly all these years, but I left because a relationship with him just would've been too much work, and I just know I was right!" or "But I stayed in the relationship all those years for the kids, and that was the right thing to do!" This is your ego now, but the more deeply you are aware that life is too precious not to follow your heart—all of the being right, being worried, and being afraid be damned—the more ego is silenced. On your deathbed, knowing with certainty there is no more tomorrow, is certainly a time that all of the truth in your heart that you did follow and should have followed will be clear. So visualize that experience now, honestly and deeply.

Then get up. You are not on your deathbed, but be aware that you, just like me and anyone and everyone else, at any moment could be. So get up! Go and do those things, try those things, have those conversations, make those moves that your deathbed experience has made you see that you need to do in order to live your truth. These are the things that matter. Get up and be who you know you really are.

Exercise 8: Do the Edgiest Thing You've Always Wanted to Do

Embrace death and dance in graceful awareness that you will assuredly meet again someday. Then bow, step respectfully away, crank the music higher, grab life, and do the wildest happy dance you've got. Literally speaking, during the one or two weeks you concentrate on this experience, embrace life with the gusto it deserves by doing one, two, or ten of the wildest, edgiest, naughtiest, most daring things you've always so badly wanted to do but were afraid to do. Come on, I know at least a few things come to mind!

I am not urging you to do anything that violates anyone else in any way or puts others at risk. Yet I am thoroughly advocating doing things that while others may proclaim them crazy or wrong, you have thought through and know are not wrong, although doing them will accomplish more than simply nudging you out of your comfort zone.

What comes to mind? Perhaps you're a man used to doing "guy things" who has, however, often secretly wondered what a pampering weekend at a spa resort would feel like. Now is the time! Perhaps you've always wanted to Jell-O wrestle, make your own erotic film, or bungee jump—or a combination of all three. Now is the time! No matter how much time you've got left, death is absolutely certain, and life is short and precious. Carpe diem. Live it.

Intense Experience #9

ᕲ

Be Like Water

We are not human beings having a spiritual experience but rather spiritual beings having a human experience.

—Teilhard de Chardin

A man has so many skins in himself, covering the depths of his heart. Man knows so many things; he does not know himself. Why, thirty or forty skins or hides . . . cover the soul. Go into your own ground and learn to know yourself there.

—Meister Eckhart

He who lives in harmony with himself lives in harmony with the Universe.

—Marcus Aurelius

Don't get set into one form, adapt it and build your own, and let it grow, be like water. Empty your mind, be formless, shapeless— like water. Now you put water in a cup, it becomes the cup. You put water into a bottle, it becomes the bottle. You put it in a teapot, it becomes the teapot. Water can flow or it can crash. Be water, my friend.

—Bruce Lee

Happiness is not beautiful swans swimming serenely on the water. Happiness is the water itself, on which the beautiful floats. And rocks that slam into the water do not break the happiness. Happiness is the water itself, within which the disturbing is absorbed.

Like your body, which it reflects, your spirit is the water. Your spirit is ever-present love and happiness. Accepting. Flowing. Giving. Connected. Always changing, always the same. Ever present, even when you are not present to it.

Whatever the circumstances, be it the most violent storm that roils and boils the water and temporarily turns it to steam or soft breezes that caress it and leave it serene, water is still ultimately and only what it is, nothing more and nothing less: it is water. So it is with your spirit.

Water, which was put here for reasons our reasoning mind cannot know, in a world and a universe that exist for reasons our reasoning mind cannot know, and serving as one with the light and the heat from fires within the earth and fires from the sun, is the source of all physical life. So it is with your spirit, the source within which your mind, body, and heart live, and which serves as one with the light and the heat of that which has been called, among other words, God, Jehovah, Allah, Yahweh, Brahman, the Universe, the One, and the Light.

Infinite Metaphors to Gain Access to Spirit

Water and the sun are metaphors, of course, just as all of the contemporary religions and belief systems and the ancient religions and belief systems that have entered the realm called mythology have their metaphors through which people have become aware of, and can embrace, the only real power, the love, the Light, God, the answer to the only real question—"Why?"—which is a question that our mere reasoning brains, no matter how much scientific research we attempt, can never know. Why are we here? Why do we exist? Why does anything exist? Your spirit is the answer; the brain and the body that your spirit is now encased in ask specific questions and want specific answers that make sense in the context of the physical sensory world we are in, but we have no explicit language for that which is beyond our sensory world. The best we can do to know and embrace spirit is through words, stories, images, music, and other metaphors, or, as in Buddhism, through the absence of them, which, of course, first still requires the human presence of them.

That we have infinite metaphors from which to choose and through which to find our way is ultimate beauty in itself. That I can look at a sunset over the mountains and feel spirit and know God is beautiful. That I can make love to a woman and feel spirit and know God is beautiful. That I can watch people hustling and bustling through the streets of downtown Chicago and notice the ants on the sidewalk hustling and bustling, too, and feel spirit and know God is beautiful. That I can hear someone's story of Jesus, Moses, Mohammed, Vishnu, Buddha, quartz crystals, or the material-world-and-nothing-more and feel someone's love and awareness through his or her story and therefore feel spirit and know God is beautiful. As long as people do not have killing or inflicting harm on others in their messages, I am passionate about and believe in all religions, all belief systems, and all lack-of-belief systems, too, because they're all human in relation to the spirit. And just because people kill in the name of religion and beliefs doesn't mean and has never meant that religion and beliefs kill people, unless the religion itself and the belief system itself specifically advocate killing. People also kill in the name of food and land, but this doesn't mean that food and land kill people. People do so often end up listening to the messenger, and that can lead to violence, but the messenger is not the message.

There are infinite metaphors to help you become aware of spirit and let it lead you so that you attain the fluid happiness that invites so much joy and beauty to come float on it, and within which all painful disturbances will still be felt but then absorbed.

Today, right now, mine is the metaphor of water. It is a rather powerful one (if I must say so myself!). Just as your spirit is always inviting me, I am inviting you to be as happy and loving as you really are, to be as deeply at peace with yourself and the world, no matter what occurs, as are the happiest and most loving people, the people who live in and act from their spirituality. Some of them are people many have heard of, such as Gandhi, Mother Teresa, Martin Luther King Jr., or Saint John of Chrysostom, who, as he was being drawn and quartered in the year 407, was noted to have said, "Praise, praise for everything. Thanks, thanks for it all." And others are people you and I have personally known whose lives may look remarkably challenging or even tragic on paper but who exude and act on love, kindness, happiness, and peace. I invite you to be like water, and if you are already like water, I invite you to be more like water. If another metaphor or a being whom you hold to be literally true, such as Jesus, works better for you in place of "water," by all means go with that.

I invite you to the most intense experience of becoming ever more aware of and living from your spirit, of being spiritual. And if you already consider yourself spiritual, then you know there is always more spiritual to be.

Before and After

All of the other Intense Experiences in this book are ultimately a means of being who you are in spirit so that you can achieve what you are meant to achieve in health, relationships, career, and all of the other markers of human life. In that sense, there aren't really nine Intense Experiences that will inevitably change your life, there is just one, but it is convenient and it evokes greater recognition if we break things down into categories. Specifically in this experience, though, you will be invited to do exercises that are variations of age-old techniques that enable you to become more aware of, and live from, your spirit.

Others who have gone through spiritual transformations can recall themselves in a before- versus an after-the-awareness sense, and although for most people it is not really an overnight thing but ongoing, I, too, can remember myself in a before versus after way.

The most succinct example I can paint for you is that I have experienced *profound* reasons to grieve four times in my life so far. I have also grieved at other times, such as for the deaths of two uncles and for my grandmother, who had to endure the pain of her sons dying, and for the death of a good friend in college. But what follows are my "big four."

The first was the death of my father, by whom I was emotionally abused for part of my childhood and with whom I had a tumultuous relationship right through his long and painful death when I was twenty. The second was my divorce from my first wife after six years of marriage, whom I got pregnant during the time of my father's dying and so asked her to marry me, and whom I raised a wonderful son with but whom I also cheated on in my young twenties. The third was the divorce from my second wife after ten years together, seven of them married. We both started our relationship practically as children, with all of our previous emotional issues still largely unresolved. This has easily been the most significant love relationship of my life to date, not only because of the number of the years but because together we both really began to grow up and into who we were in this period, and that ultimately led to an awareness that we had grown apart. It was several years into my relationship with my second wife that I recall my spiritual shift started to occur, and what would become "Intense Experiences" began to take shape. The fourth big episode of grieving happened when I was dumped and felt betrayed by a woman I had dated for only a year but with whom I had fallen deeply in love. Quite literally one night she was telling me she felt the same and was promising me forever, which she had said many times before, and then the next morning she was breaking up with me and was gone. Like dancing with joyful abandon in the street and then—boom—getting hit from behind by a Mack truck.

Always Flowing

The before version of me handled my father's death and my first divorce in the way that so many people do, in the way that makes for really juicy memoirs: with complete dysfunction. Guilt, blinding sadness, fear, and lots of anger at the world, everyone in it, and especially at myself. All of which I was barely aware of, which I was trying to fight or mask or run away from, and which was therefore in full control of me. Unchecked, it had built a thick layer of rust and crust inside me that was most certainly preventing me from being who I am, and from which I instead made plenty of self-sabotaging choices.

The after version of me is, to be accurate about it, really the during-my-spiritual-transformation version of me, because I am absolutely no saint, and there is always much more spiritual to be. This version of me handled my second divorce in a vastly different way: that is, with far less dysfunction. I still experienced the guilt, sadness, fear, and anger, but I was much more aware of these emotions. Also, I did not try to fight them with willpower or mask them with sex or positive affirmations or run from them with Nike Air Jordans. Instead, I embraced these emotions, I gave them their due attention because they are as real as the happy emotions, and I allowed them to run their course and then let them go, so that they didn't run me off my path. I was far more aware, but not entirely, for which I forgave myself every time and got right back on track.

Then the sharpest and deepest pain I have known, that of *feeling* betrayed by my girlfriend, I handled with even less dysfunction still. I stress "feeling" betrayed because, even as I was experiencing the unique searing pain of that feeling, I knew in my spirit that no other human being actually holds the power to betray another. Her intentions were not to betray, yet even in situations where one human sets out to hurt or destroy another, this person does not hold the power to betray or destroy anyone's spirit. There is a greater hand at work, I will call it God, and although God's reasons may never be known within our minds for heinous acts of violence or devastating natural disasters that strip away human life, there are still reasons. My spirit knows, and even my scientific mind that sees repeated patterns knows, that just as the smaller tragedies that do not take away our human lives are gifts in disguise to make us truer and happier in this life, the great tragedies that do take human life are given to the spirits in those humans to make them greater, wherever they may go. And after all, I did not experience a cataclysmic tragedy such as murder or torture; I was merely broken up with.

Still, even though others might look and say that the other losses I experienced were far more substantial, and in many ways they are right, the pain I experienced from this thing that felt like betrayal was the sharpest and strangest I have known. I want to stress right now that living from a spiritual base, a base of water, a base fed by ongoing Intense Experiences, does not mean I avoid pain, anger, or fear or that the moment one of these emotions arrives, I shoot it down with positive-affirmation missiles and move merrily along. These emotions are like a little child who comes to you, shaking and screaming. You do not tell that child to refocus her intentions or to "Buck up, damn it!" You accept that child into your arms, you embrace that child until the shaking and screaming subside, then off that child goes to play again. Later you may explore the greater lessons in whatever prompted those tears. Not being perfect, I may still temporarily act just like a child from pain, anger, and fear—I certainly had a short series of those after-break-up tremors with my ex-girlfriend, which ranged from promising to be her slave if she only came back, to wishing her the hottest cramped apartment in Hell. Yet the keyword here is "temporarily." Unlike the before phase of spiritual transformation, where I remained largely unaware of the emotions and so for years they moved me through life in fascinatingly self-sabotaging ways, now I had the presence of mind to quickly calm down and recognize the emotions and the actions that stemmed from them. Now I took that shaking and screaming child in my arms, and while not trying to force or wish that child's pain away, I also whispered to myself that I wouldn't let this child lead me. I simply embraced the child. I kept delving into Intense Experiences that enabled me to retain the patience, clarity, gentleness, love, and deep happiness to keep holding him—playing, deep conversations with friends and family, nature, laughter, spiritual exercises, and all of the rest. I held the child until the tears subsided, and he was okay. I knew that for a while, the child would surely run back, shaking and screaming, many times again, and I would simply repeat the cycle until it all eventually subsided—acceptance—and I was finally ready to flow on and play. I finally was, and I did.

Having a spiritual outlook gave me the eyes to see it all for what it really was: not being dumped and betrayed by a woman, but being elevated and gifted from what I will call God. I was given the gift in that relationship of great periods of clarity to see and feel deep love. Although this love will not be symbolized, celebrated, worked toward, and honored in that particular woman, and this was sad and painful, it doesn't mean the love is gone. It is always there, I feel it right now, ready to be acknowledged and acted on. In a world of more than three billion women, plenty of them single and plenty of them whom I find quite attractive, I know there is a specific woman with whom this love will be symbolized, celebrated, worked toward, and honored, and we will meet when we are meant to meet. But I do not need to wait for her to act from this amazing love; I am aware that it is the source, my source, and it can flow through me in everything I do, such as writing this book, talking with friends and family, speaking from the stage, dancing alone in my living room, and joking with waiters and waitresses. And it does. It can flow through me for myself. And it does.

"When you realize that nothing is lacking, the whole world belongs to you," wrote Lao Tzu in the *Tao Te Ching* more than two thousand years ago. And nothing is lacking still. Bad things don't happen that create a lack in your life, unless you keep allowing yourself to perceive that this is so. Rocks may fall, some mighty large and jagged, but the more like water you are, the more you will embrace the rocks, absorb the rocks, and ultimately dissolve the rocks into your Being. Love, peace, success, and happiness are not things to go fishing for; you cannot one day suddenly hook them. They are the water itself. Right now, you can envision love, peace, success, and happiness because they are already there, inside you, already yours. Now it is just a matter of choosing to love yourself and the world. It is a matter of choosing to dissolve the rusty, crusty barriers that built up inside you, blocking that love, peace, success, and happiness. It is a matter of choosing to open yourself through positive loving experiences—Intense Experiences—to who you already are and everything that is already yours. The whole world belongs to you.

Be water, my friend.

Five Intense Questions for You
1. Do you consider yourself a spiritual person? What does that mean to you?
2. What have been some of the strangest coincidences in your life? Certain things that seem too specific, with too much of a message, to be mere coincidence?
3. Whom in your personal life do you trust to advise you wisely? All friends are wonderful, but as you go deeper and become truer to who you are, it is wise to remember that people bring their own fears, insecurities, beliefs, and unresolved issues to any relationship, and although they offer you advice and counsel in love, these may well

be unintentionally loaded with their emotional baggage. Remaining aware of this is important; determining who your wisest counsels are is important. If no one comes to mind, don't worry. By opening yourself wider to who you are through the experiences in this book, your counsels will come. There are many exceptional psychologists, life coaches, spiritual guides, religious counselors, and other wise owls out there if you need them now.

4. If you are a religious person, what are your beliefs about other religions, people who don't believe in any religion, and those who don't believe in anything spiritual at all? If you are not a religious person and/or you don't believe in anything spiritual at all, what are your beliefs about religion and spirituality? From where did your beliefs come? Looking inward, is there any fear, anger, guilt, or other deep-seated emotion that might be involved in your perspective?

5. What have been the most spiritual experiences in your life so far? In which places and circumstances do you feel that you've had the clearest access to your deepest truths? Do you engage in these experiences routinely, and are you wide open to other experiences that may put you in these places and circumstances?

Be Like Water Exercises

Exercise 1: Pray, Even If

Nine out of ten Americans pray, at least sometimes. Even if you aren't religious and you equate praying with religion, separate the act from the organized systems and try praying. If you do it sometimes, try to make it a routine habit. It is a peaceful and loving way to give closure to your day before you go to sleep, so consider saying your prayers at night. Whether you are praying to God or to something for which you have no name, prayer is a beautiful opportunity to express gratitude outwardly from your heart and mind for the many gifts you have been given in life. It is an ideal opportunity to both grant and seek forgiveness, so that you are freed from those chains.

People spend their days going fast, struggling to check stuff off their endless to-do lists, and way too often focused on what they lack in their finances, jobs, relationships, and all of the rest. Prayer is a peaceful and focused reality check—an opportunity to express gratitude for the endless gifts you have and to recognize that you are actually not lacking anything. You are alive, and people you love are alive, and that is the greatest gift of all. You have a roof over your head and people who care about you. Those are some great things to begin praying about. When you start to give thanks through prayer for all of the gifts in your life, when you gently allow your perspective to shift to all that you've got, versus what you want or think you need, your life increasingly looks as rich as it is.

In a practical sense, praying provides you with a range of health benefits; this is even generally acknowledged in the scientific community, although the research on why it is clinically so is still in its infancy. A recent study also showed that when someone feels that a romantic partner has wronged him or her, prayer significantly reduces the person's vengeful thoughts and emotions. Indeed, prayer is a peaceful and focused daily opportunity to release those thoughts and emotions of anger and frustration with others who you feel have wronged you by forgiving them, and to ask for forgiveness of anyone who feels you have wronged him or her. Often these are the same people, because those we feel we've been hurt by are often those who feel so hurt by us. It is easy for us to remember who hurt us but much harder to remember those we have hurt. "Forgive us our trespasses, as we forgive those who trespass against us," as the Lord's Prayer goes; granting and asking for this forgiveness are two of the healthiest things you can do to clear the path to that loving, happy, successful person you already know deep inside you are.

Some people treat prayer as merely a request line for something they want, like calling dad from college to request some money (only the requests are often much greater: "Please let me win the lottery, God. Please, please, please!"). Yet prayer can be an ideal experience to ask for what you really need. Of course, praying in solitude is a personal thing, and you will let your praying go where it takes you, so if you are inspired to ask for specific things—that raise in salary, improved health for yourself or someone else, or an Official Red Ryder Carbine-Action Two-Hundred-Shot Range Model Air Rifle—go for it. If it feels true to you, though, consider closing your prayers by asking for clarity of perspective and a loving heart. My favorite prayer toward this end is still "The Serenity Prayer":

God grant me the serenity to accept the things I cannot change,
The courage to change the things I can,
And the wisdom to know the difference.

Exercise 2: Be Present and Meditate

Only about 9 percent of Americans meditate, but that number has been rapidly on the rise in recent years, because meditation provides such a wide range of benefits. Even if you are religious and meditation is not core to your religion, separate the act from any other belief system you may connect it to, and open yourself enough to try meditation.

Research has shown that meditation is a great way to reduce stress; for my part, I know of almost nothing else that so thoroughly eliminates stress more. Meditation is highly recommended to maintain and improve heart health, to strengthen your immune system, to decrease muscle tension, to relieve headaches, to alleviate premenstrual syndrome, and to boost serotonin levels in your body (low serotonin is associated with depression, obesity, and insomnia). For those reasons alone, it makes sense to meditate, but meditation also grants you access to the peace and happiness of your spirit self. Try it, practice it, and it will become as central to your life as eating and sleeping.

There are many meditation methods out there. As in all things, the better your instructor and the more established his or her meditation teachings, the more likely you are to reach deeper states of meditation and experience all of the benefits it can provide. Toward this end, I encourage you to visit Shambhala.org to find a highly qualified instructor near you or ask trusted sources who meditate for their recommendations.

Exercise 3: Engage Your Highest Self in the Mirror

You are lacking nothing. And that includes the wisdom inside you about how best to live your life, the path you should be on, and the rust and the crust inside that you need to dissolve. One of the most powerful exercises you can do to discover this complete inner wisdom—so that you may heed your own wise voice—is to engage your highest self in the mirror.

Consider an area of your life where you are facing challenges: perhaps in your marriage, in finding a mate, with an addiction or a health issue, or in switching careers. Stand in front of a mirror in solitude, in a time and a place where you are not worried about anyone else interrupting you. Look yourself in the eyes in the mirror. You can blink as often as you must. Don't worry, this is not a staring contest with yourself!

There will be two of you having a conversation there, looking into each other's eyes that never lie. The first will be the self whose emotions and ego may tend to keep you from truths you know should be yours and instead lead you where you know deep inside you don't want to go. The second self will be the spirit self.

The spirit self knows that fear, guilt, anger, and sadness certainly exist, but that you should never allow them to control you and keep you away from the life you deserve. The spirit self knows the difference between sensible fears, such as a fear of fire, versus fears that—afraid as you may be—are doors you need to walk through. The spirit self knows that life is precious, and there is but one life for you in this time, this place, and this body. To live according to your own truth, as scary and hard as it may sometimes seem, is the only way to live.

Face your spirit self, and, speaking out loud while looking into your eyes, define your challenge. Tell your spirit self what the challenge is and what you find so challenging about it. Tell your spirit self there in the mirror what you are afraid of, angry about, apprehensive about, and feel guilty about, as well as any and all concerns you have. Your spirit self is absolutely accepting and forgiving, so do not worry about how all of your words come out—just let them pour out.

Now switch your consciousness. Having heard the position of what we'll call your ego self regarding the challenge and all of your concerns, look your ego self in the eye and, from the consciousness of your wisest self, provide the ego self with counsel. Abiding in your spirit self now, you will have no fear of being completely honest with your ego self, even if it may hurt. Knowing that fear is a doorway, knowing that being who you really are is the truth and the happiness, guide your ego self in what to know and what to do. Always try to maintain eye contact with yourself, so that if your spirit self starts to slip into your ego self, you can pull yourself right back.

It is often astounding what you find you know that you didn't realize you knew with this exercise. As with all things, you will get better at it the more often you do it. I strongly suggest that you either audio-record your conversations with yourself or write down the results right after the conversations conclude. Then, whenever you confront the challenge you discussed, you will have that recording to keep you on track about what you know is true for you, as frightening or tough as it may be.

Exercise 4: Be Very Quiet for at Least an Entire Day

The Greek dramatist Menander noted around 300 B.C. that "Nothing is more useful than silence." And we really haven't heard from him since!

We live in a world where people sure love to hear themselves talk. There may not be nearly enough down-deep and honest talk going on out there, but there certainly is no lack of chatter, be it via texting, cell phones, Twitter, Facebook, or beyond. People are so eager to be heard, in large part because they are so deep-down lonely and feel empty, mediocre, and insignificant. Even if it is to boss their employees around or to announce how much they still love Froot Loops, people want to be heard because being heard feels like being recognized. In allowing yourself constant permission to talk, however, you severely blunt your ability to really listen to others; even more damaging, you hinder your ability to listen to yourself.

Many religions and belief systems extol the great virtue of taking vows of silence. Some practitioners take vows of silence for extended periods, for example, several weeks or a year, while others, such as the Carthusian monks, live much of their lives in silence. By ceasing to speak, they gain an enhanced ability to listen outwardly and focus inwardly on their personal beliefs.

As the American Christian monk Thomas Merton wrote, "In silence we face and admit that gap between the depths of our being, which we consistently ignore, and the surface which is so often untrue to our own reality."

You may remember many times in conversation when you were not entirely listening to what the other person was saying because you were too busy formulating what you intended to say. You cannot be fully present with others when you do this. Yet also consider how often you have spoken before you really pondered what you meant to say. In talking, we all too often show that we are not really present with ourselves. The words don't come from our deepest truths, such as love for one another, for the world, or for ourselves, but instead from ego and emotional places, such as fear, anger, frustration, and confusion. The words pour out of our mouths, and because they cannot be pulled back in, our egos want to stand by them at all costs. Whether it is complaining about the weather or passing judgment on someone else, our own words affect our moods and perspective, and our ego selves tend to want to believe the things we say, against all proof to the contrary. If I called the president of the United States a liar to my friend, then even if the president shows himself to be honest ten thousand times over, my ego wants to stand by what I said—he is a liar! If I accused a girlfriend of not really caring about me, then even if she shows that she cares about me in fifty-seven ways, my ego wants to stand by what I said—she doesn't *really* care!

Within the next week or two, plan at least one day of complete silence. Go for two days or longer if you believe you can do it; the longer you go, the more intense and beneficial the experience. Plan carefully, of course. If you work in a job where you have to talk, such as sales or news reporting, a workday is obviously not a good time for a day of silence. If you are a parent or otherwise care for someone you need to verbally communicate with, either try to spend a day away from the person or take a vow of silence except for your necessary communication with him or her.

You can decide whether your day of silence is going to be spent alone, away from friends and family, but I highly recommend that you spend your day in silence among your mature family members and friends. Of course, explain it to them so that they understand. If they give you weird looks, smile and say, "Isn't this the day you've been dreaming about, when you can say anything you want and I can't respond?" Then smile again and know that you are stepping beyond your zone of familiarity, and that's where growth and wisdom are always found. You can tell them why you intend to do it; perhaps they will be inspired to try it for themselves at some point. Most of all, ask them to respect it.

Depending on who you are, you may find this day of silence exercise surprisingly peaceful or terribly challenging. Either way, barring any true emergencies—don't allow yourself to speak for anything less—stay silent. Even if someone teases you here and there, stay silent. Focus inward. In the same way that a woman loses the sight in her eyes and becomes far more aware of other ways of seeing things, if you know you cannot speak, you will become more aware of the other ways that communication happens. You will find yourself hearing more, taking in more of what you hear, thinking about things in a different way, and processing from a deeper place, your spirit place. As always, do try to record what you discover in your journal. If you appreciate the experience, do it again but for a more extended period of time to see what you discover. Consider doing it routinely, to experience the benefits most deeply and permanently.

Exercise 5: Listen to Spirit

All great works of art that clear our internal paths to what's truly worthwhile are spiritual. For that reason, you are encouraged to delve into whatever works of literature, music, and other forms of art open you wider to your spirit.

Following are several recommendations I also encourage you to consider. Furthermore, I urge you to read the best selections from the world's great sacred texts. When you attend services of various religions and belief systems, per the exercise that shortly follows, I highly encourage you to ask religious leaders or believers which selections they most recommend from their texts to get a solid introductory understanding of their beliefs. For example, if you have never actually read more than a few passages here and there from the Christian Bible, try starting with two sections in the New

Testament, Mark and John. Mark is an easy read (compared to much of the Bible) and focuses on what Jesus claimed about himself. John, meanwhile, contains much in Jesus' own words. Read these two sections, and it will greatly enrich your understanding of our very Western culture and lifestyle, because whether or not you are Christian, these beliefs are deeply engrained in so many of our customs and habits.

The following works, meanwhile, are those that either moved me deeply or provided me with a deep awareness. I recommended them to many other people, who then lauded the power of these works as well. Experience them, and be water, my friend.

Books

The American Transcendentalists: Essential Writings, edited by Lawrence Buell. Transcendentalism is a movement that began in the nineteenth century on the East Coast of the United States and has since become a key influence on Western culture's ideas of freedom, personal responsibility, and spirituality. It stresses the inherent spirit in each individual, a spirit that "transcends" the empirical world and that is realized through intuition versus adherence to the various religions' prescriptions. Henry David Thoreau, Ralph Waldo Emerson, and Margaret Fuller are the most recognized Transcendentalists, and they are well represented in this exceptional collection, which you can dip into at any time and be deeply moved.

English Romantic Poetry: An Anthology (Dover Thrift Editions). There are few literary experiences more profoundly spiritual than reading the poetry of the greatest Romantics. Not Romantics in the lover sense or the '80s band sense, but in reference to the spiritual visionaries of the eighteenth century, such as Byron, Shelley, Keats, Blake, Wordsworth, and Coleridge. The less than $5 anthology by Dover Thrift publishing company collects some of the best.

Man's Search for Meaning, **Viktor Frankl.** In a 1991 survey by the Library of Congress and the Book-of-the-Month Club that asked readers to name a "book that made a difference in your life," this book ranked in the top ten. Frankl was imprisoned in Auschwitz and other concentration camps for five years, where his entire family, including his pregnant wife, perished, and he draws from that unimaginable experience to demonstrate how, although we cannot avoid suffering, we can cope, learn and grow from it, and live a life of deep meaning.

Peace Is Every Step: The Path of Mindfulness in Everyday Life, **Thich Nhat Hanh.** The Zen Buddhist monk Thich Nhat Hanh has written many worthwhile books, but this is perhaps his most inspiring, informative, and immediately useful introduction to Buddhist concepts. You'll find more clarity of direction in your life and greater peace and happiness with this short, joyful book.

The Prophet, **Kahlil Gibran.** One of the best-selling books in the world for good reason, it is a short masterpiece that will make your spirit flow.

The Tao of Pooh, **Benjamin Hoff.** Through brilliant and witty dialogue among Winnie the Pooh, Piglet, and their companions, the author of this short classic explains with delightful ease the concepts of Taoism, including how to live simply and in accordance with nature. Read it and then, if inspired, read the classic text of Taoism, the *Tao Te Ching.*

There's a Spiritual Solution to Every Problem, **Wayne Dyer.** I first listened to this book on audio while driving hundreds of miles through the Canadian wilderness, and that was certainly an Intense Experience. Dyer draws from many great religions and wisdom traditions, from literature, and from people's real-life stories, to convey how, with a deep commitment to self-awareness and truth, anything you can envision really is possible.

A Thomas Merton Reader. This edition showcases the Trappist monk Thomas Merton in all of his aspects: spiritual writer, poet, peacemaker, and even funny guy. A one-volume synopsis of his quest for truth, drawn from his major works and his lesser-known writings, that will have deep meaning for Christians and non-Christians alike.

Movies

First, I strongly recommend that you head to www .SpiritualCinemaCircle.com and get yourself a membership to this wonderful club, which sends you several exceptional spiritually oriented movies each month that you will almost never find in theaters. Also don't miss:

Cry, the Beloved Country. A black preacher, played masterfully by James Earl Jones, and a wealthy white landowner

---

More Spiritual Book Recommendations

An Altar in the World: Geography of Faith, Barbara Taylor Bradford

Black Elk Speaks, Black Elk and John G. Neihardt

Conversations with God: An Uncommon Dialogue, Neale Donald Walsch

Diary of a Country Priest, Georges Bernanos

The Power of Myth, Joseph Campbell

Reading Jesus: A Writer's Encounters with the Gospels, Mary Gordon

The Seven Spiritual Laws of Success, Deepak Chopra

A Simple Path, Mother Teresa

The Wisdom of a Broken Heart, Susan Piver

seem destined for violent collision. Instead, in the wake of a tragic killing, these extraordinary men form an unlikely union that represents what spirit and healing really mean.

Gandhi. This Academy Award winner for Best Picture, Best Actor, and more is a must-see. Gandhi is one of my personal heroes and certainly one of the most courageous and genuinely spiritual human beings who ever lived.

The Passion of the Christ. Mel Gibson's masterpiece telling the central story of Jesus Christ may be extremely difficult to watch at times, but no matter what your personal beliefs, it is a stunning and incredibly powerful experience.

The Power of Forgiveness. An inspiring recent documentary featuring the Amish, the Zen Buddhist monk Thich Nhat Hanh, the Holocaust survivor Elie Wiesel, and reflections from the spiritual authors Thomas Moore, Marianne Williamson, and more.

The Shift. This wonderful movie stars Wayne Dyer and incorporates his wisdom through the entertaining story of a businessman, a mother of two, and a film director. *The Shift* teaches why serving and giving back to others are among the most rewarding of all experiences and shows you how to create a life of deep meaning and purpose.

Music

Al-Mu'allim, **Sami Yusuf.** Sami Yusuf is often called the Islamic Bono because of his powerful voice and the spirit he pours into his music, and this may be his most powerful album. If you get only one song, download "Meditation."

How Sweet the Sound, **Chanticleer and Yvette Flunder.** A spirit-lifting album that takes you back to the roots of American gospel music. It contains an amazing rendition of the spiritual song of spiritual songs "Amazing Grace," but if you download individual songs, also don't miss "There Is a Balm in Gilead."

The Mask and the Mirror, **Loreena McKennitt.** This amazing album incorporates Spanish, Celtic, and Moroccan influences; poems by St. John of the Cross and Shakespeare; and Loreena McKennitt's depth, vision, and musical genius to create a powerful spiritual experience. According to McKennitt, this album asks the questions that echo down through the centuries: "Who was God? What is religion, what is spirituality? What was revealed and what was concealed . . . and what was the mask and what the mirror?"

Messiah, **Handel.** Classical composer George Frideric Handel created *Messiah* in 1741, and it is widely considered one of the, if not the, greatest choral works ever. Handel himself was a devout Christian, and the work is a profoundly soul-stirring presentation of Jesus' life and significance in the world.

The Mission Soundtrack, **Ennio Morricone.** Based on a good movie by the same name about a missionary's external and internal trials in South America, *The Mission Soundtrack* is a captivating, transformative musical experience that weaves together opulent and repeating classical themes with South American tribal influences. Light a candle in the dark, sit back in a comfortable chair and stare at the candle, and experience *The Mission.*

Su, **Mercan Dede.** *Su* is the Turkish word for "water," and water is the unifying word on this beautiful album. Featuring musical elements and guest musicians from India, Iran, the Balkans, Mediterranean Europe, and Britain, as well as Mercan Dede's native Turkey, *Su* draws on Sufi mysticism for its symbolism and just about everything else for its beats and melodies.

Tibetan Meditation Music, **Nawang Khechog.** This soothing, serene, transformative album by the renowned flutist and Tibetan monk who studied under the guidance of the Dalai

Lama was created after his recovery from a taxi accident that killed his niece and injured his son. Nawang ascribes his recovery to chanting and meditation.

Exercise 6: Refrain from What You Think You Need

Mocha lattés. *American Idol*. Football. Video games. Doritos. Diamonds. Online shopping.

People can live perfectly well without most of the things they come to believe they can't live without. That they don't have to live without them makes people fortunate in a sense; these things can certainly lend joy to living. Yet the fact that people don't actively realize they don't need any thing to live well, to be who they are, makes them unfortunate in a greater sense. It can make people dependent in ways subtle and not so subtle on things outside of themselves. People unconsciously train themselves, that is, to become dependent on things outside of themselves for something resembling happiness. And then, without an active realization that they don't need anything else to be happy, people so often end up passively skidding and crashing when those things are finally taken away or they can no longer have them. They skid and crash a little when something small that they "need" is taken away—the Dunkin Donuts on the way to their place of work closes down, or *American Idol* is finally canceled. They skid and crash a lot when something large that they "need" is taken away—another relationship with a boyfriend ends, or they lose their jobs and go bankrupt and cannot afford the luxuries that somehow became "necessities" anymore.

One of the most powerful ways you can respect your unbreakable spirit and call it forward in your life to experience happiness like water is to fast from whatever it is you think you need. This exercise does take some inner strength, but awareness is the reward, and it is well worth it. Take a week off from at least three things that may hurt you right now when you imagine a week without them. Go without what you *think* you need but *know* you really don't (so eating, for example, wouldn't qualify!). Take two weeks off if you are especially courageous and motivated to own your own life.

The braver you are about what you remove from your life, the more challenging it can be at first, but I can assure you that you will also experience a strange and profound joy and satisfaction at detaching yourself from what you think you need. In Christianity and other religions, ascetics renounce all worldly pleasures to live as close to their spirit as possible. I am not suggesting that you do so permanently, as they do, but I do strongly suggest that you try it for a week or two and periodically thereafter, to experience how you really have all that you need and don't lack for anything.

This is one of the most powerful exercises in self-awareness and self-reliance in the entire book, which is why it is also an exercise that many people want to resist. "Why should I give up having sex for a week and drinking my glass of cabernet in the evening if I don't have to?" Precisely because you don't have to, but you actively choose to. Because you know well by now that the "comfort zone" is actually a discomfort zone holding you back from awareness, growth, and the success and happiness that should be yours. As Henry David Thoreau put it, "A man is rich in proportion to the number of things he can afford to let alone."

One of the common riches that people discover with this exercise is an awareness that they don't need anything outside of themselves to make them happy. This makes sense in theory, but as you know by now, it is all about experiencing it for yourself in fact. By going through this exercise periodically, the very feeling and meaning of "losing" something changes. A "lost" girlfriend, for example, doesn't feel like the loss of self. After this exercise of doing without things they thought they needed, many people come to cherish those things for what they really are: perks. Gifts that they don't need, but gifts upon gifts to be grateful for.

Exercise 7: Journey into Different Perspectives

Recent research has found that people who attend spiritual services are 30 percent less likely to experience depression in their lifetimes. Meanwhile, those who have high levels of existential well-being are 70 percent less likely to have depression than those with low levels. ("Existential well-being" refers to a person's ongoing search for, and sense of, deep meaning and purpose in life.) Even if you doubt the existence of anything at all beyond the material world, remain open to exploring the possibilities. And even if you feel comfortable in your church, or you don't like attending church at all, make it an adventure to try exploring other churches and spiritual centers with an open and loving heart. The worst that can happen is that you will encounter a few interesting perspectives and meet some people who may become friends. The best that can happen is that you might also expand your own spiritual awareness and become more like water.

I've always found it odd that some people who are of a particular faith and who attend a particular church are afraid to visit the centers of other faiths and beliefs. How is that threatening? What kind of God would be upset that you are opening yourself to experiencing others who are finding their own ways, through other metaphors or stories they believe to be true, to love, kindness, and a better world?

There is only growth in perspective and a greater opening in the love that Jesus and other great religious figures spoke of to be had in exploring other beliefs. Sitting in on another church's or spiritual center's services is a far better way to spend a morning or an evening than wandering in circles at the mall again. So first, make a list. Which religions, churches, and spiritual beliefs are you curious to learn more about?

For uplifting jubilation, I'd like to recommend that you attend a Baptist service that includes a gospel choir. This is an amazing experience where, simply by being present, you feel spirit and you just have to clap along. If you want to experience deep peace, I recommend that you attend the services at a Buddhist temple. If you are ever in the Chicago area, go to services at the majestic architectural masterpiece called the Baha'i Temple, the primary center of worship in the United States for those of the Baha'i faith who believe in "the oneness of God, the oneness of humanity and the oneness of religion." Google "energy healing conference," and attend one such conference at least once in your life, such as the annual event in Toronto, Canada. Go to www.MeetUp.com, where you will find live discussion groups for every type of spiritual belief and practice imaginable.

Whatever new churches and spiritual services you attend, I encourage you to go there with an uncritical mind and an open heart and let yourself listen to and feel it, then talk to the people and the spiritual leaders. If they're having a potluck dinner in the basement, that's always a great opportunity to use the skills you honed in the Reveal Yourself experience to meet people and gain a deeper understanding.

Exercise 8: Discover Reverence for Everything

"When I see anything, I see everything," said twentieth-century British painter Stanley Spencer. When you see the world like that, then the world around you that you pass through every day—a world that may come to seem so ordinary and unremarkable that you stop noticing it—will become awesome and inspiring again. With eyes that see the miracle and the mystery in anything and everything, your spirit is elevated and, in a practical sense, your mood, productivity, and creativity are, too.

I invite you to choose absolutely any ordinary everyday object in your vicinity that you may have stopped noticing and revere the miracle of being through it. Look around you right now, in fact. Open your eyes a bit wider to notice the one thing in your

surroundings that may have gone unnoticed by you before. A but-
ton on your shirt? A staple remover?

Whatever it is, give it your deep consideration and attention.
For example, right now I am working in a Caribou Coffee café,
where a server brought me, hours earlier, a sample of oatmeal in
a little paper cup. Yet this is no ordinary little paper cup, because
there are no ordinary little paper cups. So many people poured
their creativity and energy into this cup: into the design, into making and running the machines that manufactured the cup, into
producing and gathering the raw materials that make up the cup.
And how much knowledge did they each draw on from still others
who put their energy into creating logos and cup designs and producing raw materials before them? As a result, how many people,
how much creativity, how much energy were actually involved
in making this cup? And what about the trees that were used
to make this cup: where did they come from and where did the
nutrients they needed to grow originate? Infinite energy and an
eternity are in this little paper cup.

Your questions, your awareness of the energy and the time
involved, can all start with a little cup for oatmeal samples or anything at all and work outward in concentric circles forever, until
you are again asking the biggest questions of all—Why are we here?
Why is anything here? Where is here? And until you are again
aware, through this seemingly mundane little cup, that all things
are connected across time and space and that as Einstein put it,
"There are only two ways to live your life. One is as though nothing
is a miracle. The other is as though everything is a miracle."

This is a very easy exercise, yet anything but a simple one: right
now and from time to time when your creativity, your perspective,
or your spirits seem dulled, pick an object and see the miracle of
you and me and everything through it. Let your questions and
imagination about that object flow and keep flowing outward,
until that grain of sand or paper cup becomes what it is, which is

one of our infinite doorways to the connectedness and the mystery and the beauty of everything.

Exercise 9: Go on a Spiritual Quest and Pack Lightly

Here we are, in the here and now, at the end of this book and the beginning of the rest of your life's journey. There is no better place to be! Perhaps you've done every exercise in this book step by step, maybe you've instead danced around and done those that most resonate with you, or you may have read this book straight through and now will go back and do the exercises. Or could you be one of those deviants who reads the ending of a book before finishing the rest of it? Naughty.

Whatever the case, I'm pulling out my presumptuous license and saying it for you: now that you're here, as stated in this book's title, you have changed. Even if you've only read through the book without yet doing any of the exercises that will deeply drive the experiences home for you, you have still experienced in your head, heart, and spirit how playing more, communicating more deeply, laughing far more, embracing death, and all of the rest inevitably change you. They don't change you into something you're not; they change you away from everything you are not into who you know you really are.

What you feed your being is how you will be. Feed yourself a diet that is high in the experiential equivalent of Twinkies, and in your work, relationships, health, mind, heart, and spirit, you will feel like a Twinkie. Feed yourself a diet of experiences that are rich in clarity, joy, depth, challenge, laughter, kindness, revelation, and all of the other delicious, nutritious ingredients, and you will feel as peaceful, successful, happy, and complete as you are. You will experience what you envision in terms of your finances, career, relationships, and all of the other markers of life, because your path will be cleared to these things that are already yours. The key is to keep feeding your being these Intense Experiences for the rest of your life. The exercises I have provided for you are doorways in, and although you will likely want to keep doing the exercises that most appeal to you for the rest of your life, you'll surely discover others on your own that enable you to thrive, too.

After you take all of that to heart, here is the final exercise I strongly encourage you to do *after* you've gone through all or most of the other exercises in this book: go on a spiritual quest, and pack lightly. Go somewhere overnight where you'll be in peaceful solitude, such as a cottage on a lake or a bed and breakfast. Make it somewhere you've never been before, to avoid any emotional residue. Avoid places with distractions such as bars or TVs, and don't even bring books or music. Simply bring clothes, toiletries, food and drink, pens and your journal, a candle, and the following six questions written down on paper. Be aware not to pack anything that carries emotional weight, such as clothes or foods that your subconscious may associate with a person or an event. Pack lightly, in other words.

When you get to your destination, remove any potential distractions from the room, such as magazines and promotions. Be as alone with yourself as possible. When you are ready, start by meditating to clear any worries and other parasites that may have clung to you from work or home, and to calm and center yourself. Don't be concerned if more parasites—thoughts about unfinished tasks and open-ended issues—randomly pop into your head anytime during this exercise; just accept that they are there and meditate to clear them again and center yourself. When you are calmed and centered, pull out your paper with the following questions, place your lit candle near the questions, and ponder them. Plan on pondering them for many hours, with rest, bathroom breaks, food and drink, meditation, and nature walks in between as needed:

1. Who am I?
2. What do I really value in life?
3. What is worth doing to be what I value? Am I doing it?

4. What is not worth doing because it doesn't nurture what I value, even though I may be doing it?
5. What is the meaning of my life?
6. Who am I?

Yes, the first and last questions are intentionally the same. By the time you answer this question a second time, you may well have considerably different responses.

For each question, answers may pour out, or they may at first barely crawl out. In either case, be patient. Don't write anything down yet. Simply let the answers come. With "Who am I?" for example, perhaps some answers will be labels, such as "I am a mother" or "I am a spirit"; others might be confessions, such as "I am a fearful person" or "I am confused"; and yet others may perhaps be metaphorical or simply downright odd, such as "I am a lion" or "I am a Twinkie." Just let them flow. If other questions pop up in your mind related to that question, let your mind explore those, too, but be sure to find your way back to answering the original question. Only when you feel in your gut that you have answered one question thoroughly should you move on to answering the next question.

Now here comes the challenging but most necessary part. When you have completed all of the questions, take a long break to clear your mind. Eat, take a walk, nap if you're tired, meditate, and then return and answer the six questions again. Don't strain to remember what you answered the last time. If some of the same answers come, that is fine, but don't struggle to recall previous answers, no matter how profound they seemed. Just stay open, calm, focused, and let the answers flow.

In our go-go-faster-faster task-oriented society, many people aren't used to, and therefore may question, this deep and repeated rumination: "When something is done, it's done, so what's the point in repeating the questions and answers?" Yet this is no mere task. The point is that although you have all of the knowledge you need inside you, essential pieces of this knowledge can get lodged between your bones and buried in the rust and crust of years and decades of unchecked emotions, such as guilt and fear. It can take lots of patient churning to loosen these pieces of knowledge and bring them forward. You will be amazed at what comes up when you repeat answering the questions. And if you have the energy and patience after a clearing break, answer them a third time, too. Three times tends to be the charm.

When you know in your gut that you have thoroughly answered all of the questions a second time or, ideally, a third, it is now highly recommended that you sleep. Let yourself wake up naturally, with no alarms. By sleeping deeply, you will allow your unconscious self to ruminate over and process everything you brought forward. When you are awake, stretch, eat, drink, and meditate until you feel fully alive and centered.

Then write the vision statement for your life: what you intend your life to mean, the things you truly value, the principles you will live by to become what you value, and the experiences you will direct your energy toward to become what you truly value. I do not want to impart any more specific suggestions for what your vision statement should contain or how it should be structured, because at this point that might impose on you. Having the utmost love for yourself and therefore the greatest respect for crafting your life's vision statement, and having ruminated consciously and unconsciously on the six previous questions, you will find that the content and the shape you give your vision statement are what it is meant to have.

When you have written it out, review it carefully. Is it complete? Is it you and only you laying down your law? There are no other voices or outside expectations in there, right?

Be aware now that just as a nation's constitution changes as the country grows, your vision statement is open to change as you grow. Revisit this exercise from time to time to keep living your truth.

Now that you have completed your vision statement, celebrate! Jump on the bed, sing at the top of your lungs, or engage in whatever form of play calls you.

When you get home, make multiple copies of your vision statement. Frame a copy. Hang it where you will always see it. And live it.

"We are constantly invited to be who we are," said Henry David Thoreau. Every Intense Experience is a wonderful invitation in. Never settle, never let mediocrity block your way. You have everything, you lack for nothing, to do what you know you were meant to do and be who you know you really are.

Be who you are. Here. Now.

Thank You

To my editor, Thomas Miller, whose talent, experience, and perspicacity made this a far better book, thank you. And a big thank you to copy editor Patti Waldygo, production editor Hope Breeman, and the whole talented and enthusiastic team at Wiley.

To Stephanie Tade, you've gone well beyond what my greatest hopes were for a literary agent. Thank you for the remarkable skill and effort and the guidance and reassurance.

To readers of my IntenseExperiences.com newsletter, thank you for all of the kind words and suggestions throughout the years and for so enthusiastically sharing my work with others. This book wouldn't exist without you.

To Beth Bottini, thank you for the support, the memories, the laughter, the dancing and singing, the love, and for trying. To Mireya Renteria, thank you for the love and for secretly saving that thousand dollars, and I am sorry.

To Asia Borycka, thank you for embracing me, discussing with me, believing in me, and for the beautiful light you are.

Thank you, Katelynn Jacob, I love you.

Thank you, Pamela Parcey, Lisa Sbragia, Richard Steelman, Jeff Davis, Dennis Neu, Dan Rosenmann, Michael Filimowicz, Kerry Jacobson, Gina Romanello, Lea Renay, Amy Hoffman, Carolyn Brafford, Tammi Stone, Jennifer McLean, Heather Fougnier, Vishen Lakhiani, Mike Reining, Joseph Mercola, Hale Dwoskin, Marc Stockman, Mark Hyman, Arielle Ford, Eric Zorn, Gwendolyn Brooks, and my uncle Rod Forston.

Thank you to all of the schoolteachers who really cared, especially Dr. Jeffrey Chown at Northern Illinois University, Ellen O'Keefe at Von Steuben High School, and Lillian McCabe at Luther Burbank Elementary School in Chicago, who among so much more wrote on my sixth-grade essay about Benjamin Franklin that "we expect great things from you, too, Brian."

To my grandmother, Ann Banas, thank you for being the living lesson in kindness, perseverance, and patience and for being my angel on earth.

To my sister, Michelene Tunca, thank you times one hundred for all you've done throughout the years, from literally protecting me with your hands when we were young to figuratively protecting me with your heart later in life. I love you. Thank you, Han, for your heart and for caring so much and so well for my sister, and thank you, Destin and Cerek Tunca, for the love and ongoing lessons in fun.

To my son, Evihn Vaszily, when you came into this world, you became my primary motivation, but as you have grown, you have become my primary inspiration. You have kindly noted that you've learned so much from me, but believe me, I have learned far more from you. I am so proud to be your dad. I love you.

To my mom, Maryann Vaszily, the greatest sage I have ever encountered, who was always there, no matter what, who is a lot of fun to hang out with, and who also makes me delicious lasagna, thank you times infinity. I love you.

And to my dad, William Vaszily, you know how you sometimes told me when I was young that my dreams were stupid and I would never amount to much? Well, I have to admit that often drove me while I wrote this book. Now I know you didn't mean those words. I know that whenever you said that, you felt so horrible afterward. Even as a child, I could see it in your eyes when you calmed down later. And I now understand the unresolved pain inside you. I know what you really meant is that you were angry that you couldn't be who you wanted to be, and you were scared for my doing the same, and what you really wanted so dearly was for me to amount to all of the dreams I had. To become who I really am. And that's what I chose to drive me while I wrote this book.

"I'm glad you know I never meant those words, Son. Again, I'm sorry. So sorry. I'm glad you know what I really meant to say. That finally gives me peace, so thank you."

You're welcome. I just wanted to tell you that. And to tell you I finally finished the book. But now I am going to go, Dad. I trust you understand. I won't be talking to you anymore, unless I some-day meet you there on the other side. So I am going to go now.

"I understand. I'll always love you. And I want you to know one more thing, Son: I couldn't be more honored to be your father. I couldn't be more proud."

I'll always love you, too, Dad. And thank you.

Additional Resources

IntenseExperiences.com

IntenseExperiences.com has become one of the world's most popular and respected personal growth and wellness Web sites, with tens of thousands of subscribers to my free newsletter. The insights you will find there are practical, motivational, intelligent, passionate, and unique. These are insights that change people's lives for the better, and as such the free newsletter is a perfect companion to this book. You will discover:

- Ongoing new exercises for each of the 9 Intense Experiences
- Practical and inspirational articles and videos (don't miss *The 9 Timeless Secrets of Being Happy* video you'll find on the homepage)
- Recommendations of the music, films, books, art, toys, festivals, cuisine, events, and destinations that have the greatest potential to transform your life positively

Plus when you sign up for my newsletter, you will receive three free gifts, including a collection of the most popular personal growth and wellness articles ever published at IntenseExperiences.com, plus *The 201 Greatest Sayings, Quotes and Parables*, a collection by Brian Vaszily.

1World1Book.com

If you love great books and you believe in their power to improve you personally and our world collectively, then sign up for my free 1World1Book.com book club. Each month, members worldwide vote from among three choices to select one exceptional book to read and discuss. Well-known and respected people such as film stars, musicians, and spiritual leaders choose a charity, and proceeds from sales of the chosen book go to that charity. You receive exclusive insights from and interviews with these individuals, the authors of the chosen books, other related experts, and me. Plus you can interact with other 1World1Book members worldwide, which provides you some amazing new perspectives and promotes greater awareness and positive change in our world.

ᔕ

In addition to IntenseExperiences.com and 1World1Book.com, I have provided in the following section select other resources that can be a powerful part of your ongoing intense experiences journey. (The specific music, films, books, cuisine, and more that are recommended in the exercises in each of the 9 Intense Experiences are not repeated here.)

Books

***300 Unmissable Festivals and Events around the World,* Frommer's.** By design, the exercises within the 9 Intense Experiences can largely be done at home. But experiencing music, food, film, dance, nature, spirituality, and more with other people has its own unique and powerful ability to expand your self-awareness, creativity, and productivity, and so attending festivals is highly recommended. This is a wonderful guide to the best of them.

***E-Motion Picture Magic: A Movie Lover's Guide to Healing and Transformation,* Birgit Wolz.** Using movies to improve mental and emotional health, also known as film therapy, is becoming increasingly popular among therapists. This book makes it very accessible to nonprofessionals, too, and includes an index of movies that are best for specific issues being addressed.

Flow: The Psychology of Optimal Experience, **Mihaly Csikszent-mihalyi.** A groundbreaking book on why achieving a state of consciousness called "flow" makes experiences rewarding to you, and an explanation of how to achieve this state.

Great Botanic Gardens of the World, **Sara Oldfield.** Few places close to high-population regions are as peaceful and inspiring as botanical gardens, and this beautifully photographed book showcases sixty of the world's finest.

The How of Happiness: A Scientific Approach to Getting the Life You Want, **Sonja Lyubomirsky.** Based on research the author and psychology professor led with thousands of people, this is one of the best positive psychology books on how to increase your daily happiness.

How We Decide, **Jonah Lehrer.** Drawing from recent discoveries in neuroscience, this book is an excellent guide to overcoming certain tendencies of our brains so we can make the best decisions in life.

Play: How It Shapes the Brain, Opens the Imagination, and Invigorates the Soul, **Stuart Brown, M.D., and Christopher Vaughan.** Based on extensive research, the founder of the National Institute for Play demonstrates that play is key to overcoming emotional obstacles and achieving success for adults.

Sacred Places of a Lifetime: 500 of the World's Most Peaceful and Powerful Destinations, **National Geographic.** A visually stunning guide to many of the world's most inspiring places with spiritual connections from ancient times to the present.

Timeless Toys: Classic Toys and the Playmakers Who Created Them, **Tim Walsh.** Beautifully written and designed, this may be one of the most joyful, interesting, and motivating books you ever read.

Us: Transforming Ourselves and the Relationships That Matter Most, **Lisa Oz.** An exceptional book on improving the relationships that matter most in your life.

Web sites

www.adta.org. The American Dance Therapy Association Web site includes a tool to help you find a therapist who uses dance and movement to improve your mental and emotional health.

www.ArtTherapy.org. Visit the American Art Therapy Association Web site to search for therapists worldwide who use the creative process to improve your mental and emotional health.

www.AuthenticHappiness.com. The Web site of Dr. Martin Seligman, the "father of positive psychology," offers useful and revealing questionnaires, such as one that measures your tendency to understand and support other people and another that measures your optimism about the future.

www.BestComedyOnline.com. If you can't head out to experience the unparalleled laughter of a live comedy club, visit this site, which offers free videos of some of the best new comedians and their routines.

www.GoodSearch.com. You search the Internet anyway—why not use this search engine, which donates 50 percent of its sponsored search revenue to a charity that you can choose?

www.LostatEMinor.com. An endlessly interesting Web site featuring brilliant contemporary photography, art, food, design, music, and much more.

www.Louvre.fr. This expansive and well-organized Web site of the Louvre, arguably the world's greatest art museum, lets you magnify masterpieces such as the Mona Lisa in high resolution, among many other features.

www.MeetUp.com. Fashion? Building your business? Meditation? Raising children? Cooking? Whatever your passions or hobbies, this free online service enables you to find people in your area who share your interest. Join a group or start your own!

www.NationalGeographic.com. One of the world's best magazines also provides one of the world's most fascinating and inspiring Web sites. It includes the breathtaking photography and informative articles on nature and travel you'd expect, but also a music section presenting amazing songs, performers, and events from across the world as well as free downloads.

www.SpiritualCinemaCircle.com. Each month, this wonderful club sends you several of the most mind-opening and inspirational films being made today on DVD.

Index